HORNBY
magazine yearbook

Selling your model railways?

Warwick and Warwick have an expanding requirement for early to modern collections of British and Foreign trains and train sets from large accumulations to items of individual value. Our customer base is increasing dramatically and we need an ever larger supply of quality material to keep pace with demand. The market has never been stronger and if you are considering the sale of your collection, now is the time to act.

FREE VALUATIONS - We will provide a free, professional valuation of your collection, without obligation on your part to proceed. Either we will make you a fair, binding private treaty offer, or we will recommend inclusion of your property in our next public auction.

FREE TRANSPORTATION - We can arrange insured transportation of your collection to our Warwick offices completely free of charge. If you decline our offer, we ask you to cover the return carriage costs only.

FREE VISITS - Visits by our valuers are possible anywhere in the country or abroad in order to assess more valuable collections. Please phone for details.

ADVISORY DAYS - We are holding a series of advisory days in all regions of the UK, please visit our website or telephone for details

EXCELLENT PRICES - Because of the strength of our customer base we are in a position to offer prices that we feel sure will exceed your expectations.

ACT NOW - Telephone or email Richard Beale today with details of your property.

LIVE BIDDING
Available on **www.easyliveauction.com**

Get the experts on your side!

Warwick & Warwick
AUCTIONEERS AND VALUERS
www.warwickandwarwick.com

Warwick & Warwick Ltd., Chalon House, Scar Bank, Millers Road, Warwick CV34 5DB England
Tel: **(01926) 499031** • Fax: **(01926) 491906**
Email: **richard.beale@warwickandwarwick.com**

Remember we supply
Switches, LEDs, Connectors and much more
Visit: www.dmgelectech.co.uk

The controller from ANE Model that does it all

THE LD101

only £129.99

New! 8 Amp power booster Now in stock works with any DCC system. £85.99

3 year warranty*

Gift Cards
Available online

New Lighting Additions

Belisha Beacons
OO/HO Guage
Pack of 2 £11.99
Pack of 2 (with module) £14.99

We also sell screws and fasteners in all sizes

Miniature Plug and Sockets (10 pack)
Single Row
2 pin £5.50
3 pin £5.50
4 pin £5.50
5 Pin £7.00

Wire Sold in 10m and 100 m
1/06	£1.60	£11.95
10/0.1	£1.50	£12.50
7/0.2	£1.60	£11.40
16/0.2	£2.30	£17.99
24/0.2	£3.29	£26.25
32/0.2	£4.50	£38.00

Globe Wall/Decorative Lights
OO/HO Guage
Pack of 5 £4.99

Yard and Area lamps
(adjustable height)
OO/HO Guage
Pack of 5 £7.25

Street lighting and Trackside Lighting available online from £6.99 a pack

Micro Connectors 2 pin
(Many uses including N Guage)
10 Pack £5.50

Multicore Cable
18 core 0.22 cable
1m £3.40
100m £64.00

Round Lantern Wall/Decorative Lights
OO/HO Guage
Pack of 5 £4.99

1960 Circular Street Lights
OO/HO Guage
Pack of 5 £7.49

New Lighting Distributor Module
This clever little PCB makes using LED lighting simple you chose the way to wire the boards can be daisy chained for differing outputs. (supplied with connection pack) **Only £12.75**

Follow us on Facebook
www.Facebook.com/modelrailwayelectronics

Ribbon, 3 Core and Ultra Fine Wire available online

We also supply
• Diodes
• Relays
• Capacitors
• Sensors
And much More!!

Remember quality components at affordable prices.

www.dmgelectech.co.uk

DMG Technical Ltd - Tel: **02920 813136**
Unit 10, Glan-Y-Llyn Ind Est, Cardiff Road, Taffs Well, CF15 7JD
Email: sales@dmgelectech.co.uk

Fast Efficent Service
P & P only £3.95
Free on orders over £100

Orders received before 2.00pm dispatched same day

*see website for details

WANTED

Model Railway & Collectables

Top Prices Paid

For all makes, all gauges and live steam, aeroplane kits, boats, die cast etc.

Instant cash paid

Will travel to collect

email: littleworthmodels@gmail.com

01775 630385
07578 708785

**Woodgate Cottage
New Road,
Deeping St Nicholas,
Spalding, Lincs, PE11 3DU**

CONTENTS

What's inside...

07 WELCOME
What a year it has been! Editor Mike Wild looks back on the remarkable developments of 2023 and introduces the key content of our action-packed 2024 yearbook.

08 REVIEW OF THE YEAR 2022-2023
The ready-to-run scene has grown massively once again. From North Eastern Railway Bo-Bo centre cab electrics to LMS 'Turbomotives' in 'OO', to LNER 'J50s' and BR 'Co-Bos' in 'N', we've got it all covered.

18 HARDWICKE AND THE 'COMPOUND'
The high-gloss finish of locomotives working main-line steam specials is unique, but difficult to capture in model form. Using the simplest techniques imaginable, Tim Shackleton recreates the look of polished 'perfection'.

26 THE FIRST AMERICAN INVASION
Most of us know of the wholesale introduction into this country of American-designed locomotives during the 1990s, but fewer are aware of the influx of around 1,000 locomotives during the Second World War. We delve into the histories of Bachmann's USA tank and Rapido's forthcoming S160.

34 FLYING SCOTSMAN IN THE 21ST CENTURY
Hornby's well-regarded Gresley 'A3' Pacific is an ideal basis for super detailing. Not content with just one *Flying Scotsman*, Richard Hall adapts three, showcasing its various conditions since 2000.

44 CHANGE FOR TITFIELD
Ealing Comedy The Titfield Thunderbolt must rank as the most modelled railway film set. *Hornby Magazine* reflects on why it is so well loved and the new ranges of ready-to-run models it has inspired.

48 MAKING TRACKS – THE GRAND CHALLENGE
The stage was set for the greatest challenge yet for Pete Waterman and the Railnuts to put together the biggest portable 'OO' gauge model railway for one weekend at the 2023 Great Electric Train Show. Discover how it was done as we take you behind the scenes.

58 MASTERPIECES IN THE GALLERY
From Southern Region steam to 1980s diesels and back to Midland Railway steam locomotives, our lavishly illustrated Gallery showcases the very best photography of the best layouts from the past year.

72 NORTH LIGHT FACTORY BACKDROP
North Light factories are a classic railway backdrop and the Key Model World Shop offers an exclusive laser-cut PJM Models kit for 'OO' gauge. Dan Evason tackles the two four-bay and a single-bay entrance kit to create an authentic façade.

78 BUILDING A LEGEND: THE GRESLEY 'P2' 2-8-2
Modern design methods and a brand-new workshop are helping to shape construction of Britain's most powerful steam locomotive. *Hornby Magazine* meets A1 Steam Locomotive Trust Chairman Steve Davies MBE in Darlington to discover how the mammoth project to scratch-build a 'P2' 2-8-2 is advancing.

www.keymodelworld.com

CONTENTS

86 ROUTE 66
One of the most recognisable locomotives currently at work in the UK is the Electro-Motive built Class 66, a type that originated in the USA and which has come to dominate our freight scene. Evan Green-Hughes celebrates 25 years of success.

94 BREAKING THE MOULD!
They were the rarest of diesels and until relatively recently unheard of in ready-to-run model form. We chart the weird and wonderful early BR-era prototype locomotives, in full size and miniature.

100 'FELL' UPGRADES
KR Models' 'OO' gauge replica of the unique 'Fell' 2-D-2 diesel-electric made its debut in autumn 2022. Using an original BR black version, Mike Wild shows how a simple capacitor upgrade can enhance its performance alongside a weathered finish.

106 TWELVEMILL BRIDGE
'TT:120' is only just getting started, but the *Hornby Magazine* team have wasted no time in getting stuck into their new challenge; to build a 60ft-square layout in this exciting new scale and which has already made its debut on the exhibition circuit!

118 FORWARD TO 2024
It is set to be another busy year of new rolling stock releases… We preview what's expected to hit the shelves during 2024.

Main image: One of the biggest stories of 2023 has been the centenary celebrations for 'A3' 60103 *Flying Scotsman*; a locomotive immortalised in thousands of models. See pages 34-41 to learn how you can individualise your own for the millennium onwards.

Above: Customise a factory unit backdrop using our exclusive northlight building kit read the full feature on page 72.

Who did it?

ISBN: 9781802829419
Editor: Nick Brodrick
Publisher, Modelling: Mike Wild
Senior editor, specials:
Roger Mortimer
Email: roger.mortimer@keypublishing.com
Design: Panda Media
Cover design: Steve Donovan
Advertising Sales Manager:
Brodie Baxter
Email: brodie.baxter@keypublishing.com
Tel: 01780 755131
Advertising Production:
Becky Antoniades
Email: rebecca.antoniades@keypublishing.com

SUBSCRIPTION/MAIL ORDER
Key Publishing Ltd, PO Box 300, Stamford, Lincs, PE9 1NA
Tel: 01780 480404
Subscriptions email: subs@keypublishing.com
Mail Order email: orders@keypublishing.com
Website: www.keypublishing.com/shop

PUBLISHING
Group CEO & Publisher: Adrian Cox
Published by
Key Publishing Ltd,
PO Box 100, Stamford, Lincs, PE9 1XQ
Tel: 01780 755131
Website: www.keypublishing.com

PRINTING
Melita Press, Paola, Malta

DISTRIBUTION
Seymour Distribution Ltd, 2 Poultry Avenue, London, EC1A 9PU
Enquiries Line: 02074 294000.

We are unable to guarantee the bona fides of any of our advertisers. Readers are strongly recommended to take their own precautions before parting with any information or item of value, including, but not limited to money, manuscripts, photographs, or other information in response to any advertisements within this publication. © Key Publishing Ltd 2023 All rights reserved. No part of this magazine may be reproduced or transmitted in any form by any means, electronic or mechanical, including photocopying, recording or by any information storage and retrieval system, without prior permission in writing from the copyright owner. Multiple copying of the contents of the magazine without prior written approval is not permitted.

Welcome

It hardly seems like five minutes ago that I was writing the Welcome to the 2023 *Hornby Magazine Yearbook*. The past 12 months have been another exciting and vibrant time in British railway modelling with a huge number of new releases, amazing and unexpected model announcements and the culmination of three year's work to create the biggest portable 'OO' gauge model railway at the 2023 Great Electric Train Show.

As you will read in our Review of the Year, there have been 100 new model releases over the past year – and that doesn't include accessories, buildings or kits – covering everything from the ever-popular English Electric Class 37s through to the compact but powerful GWR '15XX' 0-6-0PTs and even the unthinkable: a ready-to-run LMS 'Turbomotive' 4-6-2.

The diversity of the locomotives and rolling stock being offered shows just how vibrant this hobby is. It is full of life and the manufacturers behind each product work tirelessly to create models to the highest standards possible, no matter what scale or gauge you are considering.

The 2023 Great Electric Train Show showed the rise in popularity of the model railway hobby, helped greatly by the work of Pete Waterman and the Railnuts to raise its profile each summer at Chester Cathedral as well as through a new TV series – Little Trains and Big Names – which aired on More 4 during October and early November. The result was that the Great Electric Train Show was the busiest ever as crowds flocked to Milton Keynes to see the 152ft monster layout that Pete and the team had assembled for the weekend. It really was a sight to behold.

Naturally there were many more layouts to see at the show – including the debut of our brand-new 'TT:120' scale layout Twelvemill Bridge - as well as a huge line up of trade stands making it an unmissable weekend. To everyone who came thank you for joining us at the 2023 Great Electric Train Show - roll on 2024!

This Yearbook has brand-new features that you won't find anywhere else including the full behind the scenes story of the Making Tracks Grand Challenge layout build alongside step by step modelling guides from our dedicated modelling team, historical features about the American influence on British railway locomotive design in the steam and diesel eras plus our annual Review of the Year and Forward to 2024 surveys which bring together all the arrivals and announcements across the scales.

We also have a full modelling guide for *Flying Scotsman* to close its centenary year as well as the latest on construction of the all new Gresley 'P2' 2-8-2 from the A1 Steam Locomotive Trust and the models that have been created by Hornby.

We hope you enjoy all the features in our sixteenth Yearbook and that they inspire you to continue your model railway journey or start out on the project you have always wanted.

Happy modelling!

Mike Wild
Publisher, Modelling

The 2023 Great Electric Train Show was the busiest ever as crowds flocked to see Making Tracks: The Grand Challenge – all 152ft of it. Jonathan Newton.

Review of the Year 2022-2023

Another incredible year has passed with more than 100 new products completed. **MARK CHIVERS** takes a detailed look at what's appeared during the past 12 months.

It has been another astonishing year for new model releases with a steady stream of new projects coming to fruition – 106 in total across 'OO', 'N', 'O', 'OO9' and, now of course, 'TT:120', which appears for the first time with all-new products in this new scale.

In addition to the traditional annual catalogue launch from Hornby and the quarterly British Railway Announcements from Bachmann, most manufacturers have adopted a series of ad-hoc project announcements across the year, some coinciding with major events such as model railway exhibitions. This has resulted in an even spread of new projects being announced across the year.

Looking a little closer at this year's release figures, 57 of the projects completed were 'OO', 20 were 'O' gauge, 12 were 'N', nine were 'TT:120' and eight were 'OO9'. Of these, there were 23 'OO' gauge locomotives, 27 'OO' wagons and seven 'OO' carriage projects (although note that several of these projects spawned multiple vehicle types). 'O' gauge modellers saw seven new locomotives, 11 new wagons and two new carriage projects completed, while for 'N' gauge, there were five new locomotives and seven wagon projects that came to market. Three new 'OO9' locomotives appeared too.

Hornby's new 'TT:120' scale range spawned nine new projects with three locomotives, four wagon and two carriage projects within 12 months of the new range's announcement last October together with the first train sets. Individual 'TT:120' scale items began to appear from the second quarter of the year. Indeed, the first *Hornby Magazine* review samples arrived in May. Since then, the two steam locomotive types and a Class 08 diesel shunter have been released in multiple liveries, together with carriages, wagons and accessories for the scale – plus the train sets have reappeared with Hornby's new factory-fitted Bluetooth Triplex Sound system.

LOCOMOTIVES

Our survey begins, appropriately, with one of the earliest steam locomotives, the Liverpool and Manchester Railway's (L&MR) 0-4-2 *Lion*, produced in 'OO' by Hornby which arrived for review in October 2022. This delightful locomotive is one of two projects modelling the L&MR's historic locomotive which went on to find fame as a star of the big screen, thanks to a starring role in the Ealing comedy *The Titfield Thunderbolt* (see page 44). Hornby's all-new 'OO' gauge model certainly captures the look of the real thing with a stunning timber effect paint finish to the boiler barrel and eye-catching brass bands. It features a three-pole motor and a factory-fitted 15mm x 11mm cube speaker in the tender. Just five months later *Lion* was joined by *Tiger*, which was added to the Hornby range as part of the 2023 catalogue launch in January. It appeared in later condition following rebuilding and featured a stovepipe chimney, plain black topped firebox and a slightly more subdued livery than that carried by *Lion*. As with other models in the range, it is also supplied with a set of pre-painted footplate crew.

In between these releases, Hornby delivered an altogether more modern 'OO' gauge project; a newly-tooled model of the Class 43 High Speed Train power cars. Our review samples included a First Great Western 'fag packet' liveried pairing, together with examples in East Coast, GWR and Locomotive Services Limited 'Midland Pullman' liveries. Close inspection reveals detail differences between the models, with the LSL example fitted with an upper headlight above the cabs, modelling the latest developments on the real thing. The tooling suite also caters for different exhausts, exhaust cowls, roof fan grille styles, light clusters, cab door window variants and more. Independently powered roof fans are also included in the specification, along with a pair of twin cube speakers in each power car.

Hornby also delivered another of its new 'Hornby Dublo' models in the form of a Gresley 'A4' 4-6-2. Two models were initially produced with 4900 *Gannet* in LNER Garter blue with valances and a BR lined green version with early crests as 60007 *Sir Nigel Gresley*, the subject of our review. This super new addition to the range followed previous locomotives in the Hornby Dublo collection with a new die-cast body allied to the high-fidelity chassis and existing tender tooling. In addition, this model incorporates Hornby's new kinematic power coupling between the locomotive and tender, while it also comes with pre-painted footplate crew.

During the summer, we were afforded a glimpse of Hornby's all-new LNER 'P2' 2-8-2 at the A1 Steam Locomotive Trust's new workshop and headquarters in Darlington, where the new-build 'P2' 2-8-2 2007 *Prince of Wales* is under construction. Our review sample modelled 2007 *Prince of Wales* and was the first to arrive, with three other models also due in the first batch of releases. It features a double chimney, die-cast chassis, five-pole motor, flywheel, 21-pin Digital Command Control (DCC) decoder socket and a steam generator casing in the locomotive, alluding to a forthcoming release which is set to feature a smoke generator.

Heljan teamed-up with Rails of Sheffield and Locomotion Models to produce a range of superbly detailed NER steeple cab electric locomotives, based around the National Railway Museum's unique surviving ES1.

Coinciding with the imminent end of HSTs in daily main line service, Hornby has produced a series of power cars and matching Mk 3 carriages. One of the most striking sets is Locomotive Services' 'Blue Pullman' charter set, headed by 43046 *Geoff Drury 1930-1999*.

REVIEW OF THE YEAR

HORNBY MAGAZINE YEARBOOK 2024

Just prior to this *Hornby Magazine Yearbook* closing for press, Hornby delivered its 'OO' gauge LMS 'Turbomotive' 4-6-2, featuring a die-cast body, adding to its heft, working lamps front and rear and firebox glow. Both versions of the model were received for review in LMS and later BR condition, with detail differences incorporated into the body tooling. It also features a five-pole motor, flywheel and 21-pin DCC decoder socket.

Bachmann's 'OO' gauge release plan over the past 12 months has included several upgrades to existing models, including the BR Standard '9F' 2-10-0 and the Class 40 1Co-Co1, while its sole all-new 'OO' gauge project was in conjunction with North Yorkshire based The Model Centre (TMC). Our review samples of the stunning North Eastern Railway 'O' (London North Eastern Railway (LNER) 'G5') 0-4-4T arrived with us in June and what a delight they are. Eight different models formed the first batch of releases with detail differences between them incorporated such as to the coal bunkers – original style, bunkers with cage extensions and a cage and hopper version for increased coal capacity. There are also differences to the cab roofs, safety valves, early and late dome positioning, buffer shank types and push-pull versions with appropriate equipment. Liveries cover the extent of their operation and are produced in DCC ready and DCC sound-fitted forms.

Accurascale released several significant 'OO' gauge locomotive projects during the past 12 months, the first being its Class 92 Co-Co electric which appeared during November last year. While the previous Class 55 'Deltic' had set a new bar for its powered locomotive releases, the Class 92 raised this higher still with our digital sound fitted example featuring an ESU LokSound decoder, Accurathrash bass speaker, four capacitor stay-alive power pack and two silent motor driven pantographs which could be raised and lowered. In addition, the model featured a raft of lighting options too. Colour schemes range from BR Railfreight triple grey through to DB Schenker, GB Railfreight and Caledonian Sleeper liveries.

The company's eagerly awaited Class 37 locomotives began to appear during April, with the modernised Class 37/4 Co-Co diesels arriving first, with 20 different models set to follow in the coming months including Class 37/0s and Class 37/6s. Our review sample was of Direct Rail Services operated Class 37/4 37425 *Sir Robert McAlpine/Concrete Bob* in retro BR Regional Railways colours. The drive system on our review sample proved smooth and quiet, while the onboard digital sound system acquitted itself well too. Lighting options include subtle cab console illumination, adding to the functionality of these super new arrivals. Not surprisingly, Accurascale's 'OO' gauge Class 37 won the *Hornby Magazine* Model Railway Award for best 'OO' gauge locomotive.

In July, the next batch of Class 37s - the Class 37/0s – arrived with our review samples modelling the Scottish 'car headlight' examples, fitted with these additions during use on Scottish Highland routes in the 1980s. Four models were released, with three supplied for review finished as 37027 *Loch Eil* in BR blue, 37026 *Shap Fell* in Railfreight Distribution livery and 37051 in Railfreight Metals triple grey. 37043 *Loch Lomond* in BR large logo blue followed shortly after. As well as the distinctive car headlamp on the cab fronts, there are several detail differences incorporated.

Accurascale's next release was much different as its first 'OO' gauge steam locomotive arrived during August, with our review sample modelling 7812 *Erlestoke Manor* in BR lined green with late crests. Opening the box was a real treat as the various layers of packaging revealed this stunning model with its detailed cab interior, which even features the tip down seats – the driver's one is modelled in the down position, while the fireman's is up! Performance matched its good looks and supplied with replacement etched metal nameplates and 'Cambrian Coast

REVIEW OF THE YEAR

Express' headboards, in a nod to the prototype's regular operations on the route west of Shrewsbury. Our digital sound-fitted review model features a Next18 DCC decoder socket, three-pole motor, stay-alive power pack and an impressive level of detailing.

In September, Accurascale welcomed the next batch of its Class 37s with a selection of Class 37/6s arriving – mostly Direct Rail Services liveried examples, although there are several other examples including a Rail Operations Group liveried model and Accuracale's eye-catching web-exclusive model of Class 97 97301 in Network Rail yellow. A further batch of original Class 37/0s was due as this yearbook closed for press.

Dapol delivered a couple of 'OO' gauge locomotive projects during the year with one diesel and one steam locomotive each. The diesel project came to fruition in January with the arrival of the Class 59 Co-Co diesel. These large diesel locomotives were the first privately-owned diesels to operate on BR metals in the 1980s on aggregates trains for Foster Yeoman and ARC initially. Dapol's new models included examples in these colour schemes as well as National Power and DB Schenker traffic red. Models are available DCC ready, DCC fitted and DCC fitted with a smoke generator. This was the first 'OO' gauge ready-to-run model to be released with a 'diesel' smoke generator, which automatically emitted exhaust during the first ten seconds of operation. Versions fitted with a smoke generator and DCC sound were also produced as exclusives through Dapol's website.

Dapol's second 'OO' gauge locomotive during the year was a collaboration with Rails of Sheffield in the South Eastern and Chatham Railway 'D1' 4-4-0, first announced in February 2022. Six models have been released in SECR wartime grey, Southern Railway olive green (x2), BR lined black with early crests, BR lined black with late crests and British Railways black with Bulleid sunshine lettering. The models featured an outstanding level of detailing »

Main: One of the most highly-detailed steam locomotives to ever appear in 'OO' ready-to-run form, Accurascale's Collett 'Manor' has been one of the year's most popular releases. This is the preserved 7812 *Erlestoke Manor* – its prototype splits its time between the Severn Valley and West Somerset railways.

Top right: Both Bachmann and Accurascale have delighted modellers with all new ranges of the household Class 37. Pictured are the latter company's Regional Railways 37425 *Sir Robert McCalpine/Concrete Bob* and InterCity Mainline 37419 *Carl Haviland 1954-2012*.

2022-2023 NEW READY TO RUN LOCOMOTIVES

MODEL	SCALE	MANUFACTURER	RELEASED	FEATURED
L&MR 0-4-2 Lion	'OO'	Hornby	October	HM186
Kerr, Stuart 'Victory' 0-6-0T	'OO'	Planet Industrials	October	HM186
Mainline Hunslet 0-4-0ST	'OO9'	Bachmann	November	HM187
NER ES1 electric	'OO'	Heljan/Locomotion/Rails	November	HM187
BR Class 92 Co-Co	'OO'	Accurascale	November	HM187
BR Class 26 Bo-Bo	'O'	Heljan	December	HM188
BR Class 27 Bo-Bo	'O'	Heljan	December	HM188
BR Class 43 HST power cars	'OO'	Hornby	December	HM188
Quarry Hunslet 0-4-0ST	'OO9'	Bachmann	January	HM189
BR Class 28 Co-Bo	'N'	Rapido Trains UK	January	HM189
BR Class 59 Co-Co	'OO'	Dapol	January	HM189
Hunslet 16in 0-6-0ST	'OO'	Rapido Trains UK	February	HM190
BR Class 90 Bo-Bo	'N'	Graham Farish	March	HM191
L&MR 0-4-2 Tiger	'OO'	Hornby	March	HM191
GCR 'A5' 4-6-2T	'OO'	Sonic Models	March	HM191
LNER 'A4' 4-6-2	'OO'	Hornby Dublo	April	HM192
Ruston 165DE shunter	'OO'	Heljan/Kernow/Bauer	April	HM192
BR Class 37/4 Co-Co (mod)	'OO'	Accurascale	April	HM192
Wickham Type 27 trolley	'O'	Ellis Clark Trains	May	HM193
LNER 'A4' 4-6-2	'TT:120'	Hornby	May	HM193
LSWR 'B4' 0-4-0T	'O'	Dapol	June	HM194
LNER 'G5' 0-4-4T	'OO'	Bachmann/TMC	June	HM194
LNER 'J50' 0-6-0T	'N'	Sonic Models	June	HM194
LSWR 'M7' 0-4-4T	'N'	Dapol	June	
SECR 'D1' 4-4-0	'OO'	Dapol/Rails	July	HM195
LNER 'A1'/'A3' 4-6-2	'TT:120'	Hornby	July	HM195
LNER 'P2' 2-8-2	'OO'	Hornby	July	HM195
NBL Prototype Bo-Bo 10800	'OO'	Heljan	July	HM195
BR Class 37/0 Co-Co	'OO'	Accurascale	July	HM195
L&MR 0-4-2 Lion	'OO'	Rapido Trains UK	August	HM196
Mainline Hunslet 2-4-0STT	'OO9'	Bachmann	August	HM196
BR Class 08 0-6-0	'TT:120'	Hornby	August	HM196
BR Class 58 Co-Co	'O'	Heljan	August	HM196
GWR 'Manor' 4-6-0	'OO'	Accurascale	August	HM196
GWR streamlined railcar	'O'	Dapol	August	
GWR parcels railcar	'OO'	Heljan	September	HM197
WR '15XX' 0-6-0PT	'OO'	Rapido Trains UK	September	HM197
BR Class 73 Bo-Bo	'O'	Heljan	September	HM197
BR Class 37/6 Co-Co	'OO'	Accurascale	September	
LMS 'Turbomotive' 4-6-2	'OO'	Hornby	October	HM198
Hunslet 'Austerity' 0-6-0ST	'N'	EFE Rail	October	HM198
TOTAL: 41				

Tiny but mighty 1: EFE Rail's 'N' gauge 'Austerity' 0-6-0ST, also produced in its 'J94' form.

from the exterior appearance to the cab interior, brimming with physical and printed detailing. Its smooth operation is aided by a five-pole motor and flywheel, although our review sample proved a little light on its feet.

Danish manufacturer Heljan delivered four new 'OO' gauge projects during the year, two of which were collaborations with retailers. The first was the North Eastern Railway steeple cab electric locomotive ES1, now part of the National Collection, produced for Rails of Sheffield and Locomotion Models. Five different versions have been produced – two for Locomotion Models in as-preserved and in 1908-1923 NER green, while Rails of Sheffield received examples as No. 1 in LNER unlined black, 26500 in BR black with early crests and 26500 in BR lined apple green with late crests, which arrived towards the end of 2022.

The manufacturer's next collaboration was with Kernow Model Rail Centre and Bauer Media with the release of the Ruston 165 0-6-0DE shunter, with examples appearing during April. Our review samples were finished as Industrial Ruston No.45 in National Coal Board green and BR Permanent Way Machine (PWM) 97653 in BR engineers' yellow, with a weathered appearance; this latter model exclusive to Kernow Model Rail Centre. The Industrial versions are offered as general release models, while the PWM examples were available through Kernow Model Rail Centre (weathered) and Bauer Media (pristine). The specification includes a Next18 DCC decoder socket, dedicated space for a speaker, detailed cab interior and separately fitted handrails.

Heljan has also carved a niche through the years with several models of prototype locomotives and during July its 'OO' gauge North British Prototype Bo-Bo 10800 arrived for review. Despite the unique status of this locomotive, Heljan has been able to produce its three main liveries: BR black with early crests and silver bogies, BR black with early crests and black bogies (in weathered or pristine finishes) and BR green with late crests.

In September, the manufacturer's fourth 'OO' gauge locomotive project arrived in the shape of the unique Great

2022-2023 NEW READY TO RUN CARRIAGES				
MODEL	SCALE	MANUFACTURER	RELEASED	FEATURED
BR Mk 1 CCT	'O'	Heljan	October	HM186
BR Mk 3 carriages	'OO'	Hornby	November	HM187
Ffestiniog Quarryman's coaches	'OO9'	Peco	November	HM187
LSWR cross-country carriages	'OO'	EFE Rail	March	HM190
Mk 5 Caledonian Sleepers	'OO'	Accurascale	March	HM190
Mk 5 TPE carriages	'OO'	Accurascale	March	HM190
GWR 'Siphon G' vans	'OO'	Accurascale	May	HM192
Pullman carriages	'TT:120'	Hornby	June	HM193
BR Mk 1 carriages	'TT:120'	Hornby	June	HM193
SR GM's Saloon/Caroline	'OO'	Revolution Trains	September	HM196
LBSCR Stroudley coaches	'O'	Dapol	September	
GWR Toplight City coaches	'OO'	Dapol	October	
TOTAL: 12				

Tiny but mighty 2: Bachmann's miniature 'Quarry Hunslets' have been a revelation in 'OO9'.

REVIEW OF THE YEAR

Tiny but mighty 3: LSWR 'B4' dock tanks supplement Dapol's expanding 'O' gauge range.

Western Railway (GWR) AEC 'Razor Edge' parcels railcar W34W. This latest release features a 21-pin DCC decoder socket, five-pole motor and two flywheels aiding its smooth quiet running characteristics.

During October 2022, just as the last issue of the Hornby Magazine Yearbook closed for press, Planet Industrials delivered its first ready-to-run 'OO' gauge steam locomotive with the Kerr, Stuart 'Victory' 0-6-0T. The impressive specification for this model included more than 200 separate parts, injection moulded detail, a die-cast boiler and high-torque motor with brass flywheel and slow-speed 40:1 gearbox. Five versions have been produced in plain black, Inland Waterways and Docks lined grey, lined green, lined maroon and plain black; the latter for Rails of Sheffield as a retailer exclusive finished as ROD608.

Rapido Trains UK delivered two new 'OO' gauge locomotive projects for review, with the first arrival appearing in January with the arrival of the Hunslet 16in 0-6-0ST. Seven general release versions have been produced in a selection of colour schemes including black, blue, green and red with unique names, markings and locomotive numbers.

For its next 'OO' gauge project, the company selected the Hawksworth '15XX' 0-6-0PT, which arrived with retailers during September 2023. Straight from the box our review sample of 1504 in BR black with late crests captures the appearance of the real things that were used on empty stock workings in and out of Paddington station during the 1950s and early 1960s. Liveries produced include BR plain black, BR black with early crests, BR black with early crests, BR lined black with early crests, as-preserved BR lined black with early crests, National Coal Board (NCB) maroon and a 'what if' GWR green example.

Finally, for 'OO' gauge locomotive projects, Sonic Models debuted its first powered model in March with the arrival of the GCR 'A5' 4-6-2T. The models incorporate die-casting for the main body elements as well as finely moulded parts for the detailing, which are sublime, while powered by a five-pole motor with brass flywheel. Our review samples were finished as 373 in Great Central Railway lined green and 69804 in BR lined black with early crests.

'N' GAUGE

Of the 12 new 'N' gauge projects that came to fruition during the past 12 months, five were locomotives: three steam outline, one diesel and one electric.

Significantly, Rapido Trains UK joined the fold with the release of its first 'N' gauge locomotive - the Metropolitan Vickers Class 28 Co-Bo. The 'spec' includes a centrally mounted motor, twin flywheels and a Next18 DCC decoder socket. Rapido Trains UK's Class 28 was voted 'N' gauge locomotive of the year in the Hornby Magazine Model Railway Awards 2023.

Graham Farish delivered its 'N' gauge Class 90 Bo-Bo electric during February, with five versions offered covering BR InterCity 'Swallow', BR Railfreight, Rail Express Systems, Virgin Trains and Freightliner Genesee and Wyoming colour schemes. The impressive specification includes a coreless motor, twin flywheels, Next18 DCC decoder socket, factory-fitted speaker, directional lighting, cab illumination and a poseable pantograph.

Dapol's new 'N' gauge London and South Western Railway (LSWR) 'M7' 0-4-4T was released during June. This latest iteration features a three-pole motor, improved power collection, together with a die-cast chassis and metal wheels.

One of the more recent entrants to 'N' gauge, Sonic Models, released its 'N' gauge LNER 'J50' 0-6-0T. Our review samples were finished in LNER lined black and BR black with late crests. On board is a coreless motor and a 6-pin DCC decoder socket.

Rounding off the year for 'N' gauge locomotive projects, EFE Rail delivered its all-new LNER 'J94'/Hunslet 'Austerity' 0-6-0ST during October. Announced as part of Bachmann's Autumn 2023 British Railway Announcements, featuring separately fitted handrails, grab handles and a decorated cab interior.

'TT:120' SCALE

Hornby's new 'TT:120' scale range launched in October 2022 and to date has spawned several all-new locomotives with Gresley 'A1'/'A3' 4-6-2s, Gresley 'A4' 4-6-2s and a Class 08 diesel shunter. The steam locomotives have flown the flag for the fledgling scale in two train sets – 'The Scotsman' and 'The Easterner' – as well as being available as separate items too.

The first train sets arrived on the market just before Christmas 2022, with further supplies arriving in mid-2023. More recently, digital versions of the train sets have appeared, with the main locomotives Gresley 'A1' 2550 Blink Bonny and 'A4' 4-6-2 60004 William Whitelaw fitted with Hornby's new Bluetooth Triplex Sound (TXS) Next18 decoders and speakers, which launched as

Tiny but mighty 4: Hornby's first diesel locomotive in its new 'TT:120' scale is the Class 08.

part of the company's 2023 catalogue launch in January. Since then, some of the planned locomotives have gained a Triple Sound fitted option, such as Gresley 'A4' 4468 Mallard in LNER garter blue. The 'A4' was voted 'TT:120' locomotive of the year in the *Hornby Magazine* Model Railway Awards.

At the other end of the scale, a diminutive Class 08 diesel shunter was released in several colour schemes – BR blue, DB red and GB Railfreight orange and blue. It featured a three-pole motor, 6-pin DCC decoder socket and bags of character.

'O' GAUGE
Those modelling in 'O' have enjoyed another outstanding year with seven new locomotives appearing – four from Heljan, two from Dapol and something a little different from Ellis Clark Trains.

Heljan has released the lion's share with the Class 26 and 27 Bo-Bo diesel arriving in December 2022. These Scottish stalwarts feature two five-pole motors (one per bogie), all-wheel drive and large brass flywheels. These were followed later in the year by a Class 58 and a Class 73 electro-diesel. Both are standout models, with the latter representing Heljan's new generation of models that aim to set a new benchmark for 'O' gauge locomotives. It features more than 550 separate parts, powered roof fan and eight switchable lighting functions.

Dapol's range of 'O' gauge motive power continued to expand during the year with two very different projects appearing with retailers in the LSWR 'B4' 0-4-0T and GWR streamlined diesel railcar. The 'B4' built on the success of the company's 'OO' gauge model and features a five-pole motor, 21-pin DCC decoder socket, firebox flicker, separately applied detailing and (initially) offered in six identities. For GWR modellers, the streamlined railcar is also a delight with its smoothed, rounded edges and exceptional detailing – even the seats feature printed moquette. The specification includes a heavy die-cast chassis, low-profile five-pole motor, all-wheel pick-up, 21-pin DCC decoder socket, directional lighting, interior illumination and sliding luggage doors.

For something a little special, Ellis Clark Trains carried the baton for 'O' gauge with the release of its delightful Wickham Type 27A inspection trolley – a deserved winner of a *Hornby Magazine* Model Railway Award. In spite of the size and openness of this model, the mechanism is completely hidden from view and the level of detail is superb, especially the bench seating and controls. It features a coreless motor and Next18 DCC decoder socket, offered DCC ready or DCC sound-fitted.

'OO9' GAUGE
This year has seen another burst of energy for the 'OO9' modeller with three new ready-to-run locomotives appearing on the scene from Bachmann.

First to appear was the Penrhyn Quarry Mainline Hunslet in original 0-4-0ST form, with three versions offered as Charles in lined black with early sanders, Blanche in lined black and no sanders, and Linda in weathered black with later sanders. Each features a coreless motor, Next18 DCC decoder socket and firebox flicker. These were followed by the tiny 58mm long Quarry Hunslet 0-4-0STs a month or two later. The delightful Quarry Hunslet was voted best 'OO9' locomotive in the Hornby Magazine Model Railway Awards.

Later in the year, Bachmann revealed the first version of the Ffestiniog Mainline Hunslet 2-4-0STT as *Linda* in Ffestiniog Railway midnight blue as a Bachmann Collector's Club limited edition. In October 2023, Bachmann also announced that two further versions of the Ffestiniog Mainline Hunslet 2-4-0STTs were set to appear in their present-day coal-firing condition in Ffestiniog Railway lined green as *Blanche* and *Linda*.

CARRIAGES
Looking to rolling stock, 12 new carriage projects were completed during the year – seven for 'OO', two for both 'O' and 'TT:120' and one for 'OO9'. There were no 'N' gauge carriages during the period under review although as this issue of the *Hornby Magazine* Yearbook closed for press Revolution Trains' all-new 'N' gauge Mk 5 Caledonian Sleeper carriages were arriving with retailers.

Of the seven new 'OO' gauge carriage projects completed, three were from Accurascale with newly tooled Mk5 Caledonian Sleepers carriages and TransPennine Express five-car Nova sets, followed later in the year by GWR 'Siphon G' bogie vans.

Representing the contemporary railway scene, the 'OO' gauge Mk 5 carriages are presented in a selection of book-style sets

Dapol's 'OO' Class 59 was a welcome release in early 2023; a locomotive well overdue for the kind of detailing the modelling fraternity now expects. This is National Power 59204, which comes with working lights and smoke generator (DCC only).

REVIEW OF THE YEAR

Rainbow Railways' exclusive green liveried BR(S) General Manager's Inspection Saloon is a new Revolution Trains' tooling for 'OO'.

representing the 'Highlander' and 'Lowlander' sleeper trains operated by Caledonian Sleeper with Glasgow and Edinburgh portions, along with Aberdeen, Inverness and Fort William sections offered in packs containing four or six vehicles to make up realistic formations (as portions or in full). The outstanding models really do look striking with four vehicle types produced – Club Cars, Seated Cars, Sleeper Cars and Accessible Sleeper Cars. Each are neatly decorated in the company's eye-catching colour scheme along with smoked glazing, detailed underframes and interiors, separate destination panels for customer fitment, interior illumination and working taillights, both of which can be switched on and off with a magnetic wand device.

The company's 'OO' gauge Mk 5 TransPennine Express 'Nova 3' five-car sets also arrived with similar presence, thanks to their distinctive colour scheme and the unique Driving Trailer vehicle for these push-pull sets. Again, detailing is superb inside and out, while the complicated livery is beautifully presented.

For its next release, Accurascale turned the clock back for its collection of GWR 'Siphon G' bogie vans covering Diagrams O.33, O.59, M.34, O.62 and O.62r, from original GWR brown examples to those in BR blue Newspaper guise in the final years of revenue earning service. A departmental green version is also offered as an Accurascale Exclusive edition.

Having revised its InterCity 125 High Speed Train power cars, Hornby introduced a new collection of 'OO' gauge Mk 3 carriages to match in late 2022. They featured all-new body tooling, correct roof arrangement with fine grab handles, flush glazing, neatly moulded bogies and super livery applications. Among the first to arrive was a full set of vehicles in First Great Western 'Fag Packet' livery, with unique running numbers.

Bachmann's EFE Rail brand once again teamed up with Kernow Model Rail Centre to introduce all-new 'OO' gauge LSWR cross-country carriages in early 2023. These were offered as three-car sets initially (four-car sets followed later in the year) formed as a Composite and two Brake Third vehicles. These are formed as authentic three car sets finished in SR malachite green, BR crimson and BR (SR) malachite green and featured a wealth of separately applied detailing.

Meanwhile, Revolution Trains' long-awaited 'OO' gauge BR Southern Region General Manager's Inspection Saloon arrived during the summer, with two BR versions offered in blue and grey and Network SouthEast colours, together with two later variants finished in 'Viridian' green (a Rainbow Railways exclusive) and Brunswick green – these latter two models also carrying *Caroline*

The Hornby Magazine 'TT:120' carriage of the year is Hornby's Pullman.

nameplates, reflecting its later post-privatisation career to date.

Finally for 'OO', just as we closed for press, Dapol's all-new GWR 'Toplight' City coaches arrived for review, with samples representing a Brake Second, Composite and All Second in BR crimson. Each is very neatly finished with frosted toplight glazing, impressive interior detailing, heavy die-cast chassis and bogies, together with interior illumination and a working tail lamp on the Brake Third.

'TT:120' SCALE

When Hornby launched its new 'TT:120' range in October 2022, two carriage types were revealed, initially with a selection of Pullman cars and BR Mk 1 coaches planned for the first tranche of releases. The Pullman cars include a First Kitchen with several names offered, together with a Third Class Brake Parlour Car, while the BR Mk 1s included »

2022-2023 NEW READY TO RUN WAGONS

MODEL	SCALE	MANUFACTURER	RELEASED	FEATURED
14 ton anchor-mounted tanks	'O'	Dapol	October	HM186
LSWR Diagram 1410 vans	'O'	Kernow MRC	October	HM186
JNA/MMA bogie box wagons	'N'	Revolution Trains	October	HM186
HAA MGR coal hopper wagons	'OO'	Cavalex/Trains4U/KMS	November	HM187
MHA open ballast wagons	'OO'	Accurascale	November	HM187
SECR 10 ton covered vans	'OO'	Rapido Trains UK	November	HM187
SECR 12 ton ballast wagons	'OO'	Rapido Trains UK	November	HM187
Seven-plank open wagons	'N'	Peco	December	HM1088
Ecofret container flats	'OO'	Revolution Trains	December	HM188
IPA car carriers	'OO'	Revolution Trains	December	HM188
Conflat-P container flats	'N'	Rapido Trains UK	January	HM189
RNAD box vans	'OO9'	Bachmann	January	HM189
RNAD flat wagons	'OO9'	Bachmann	January	HM189
RNAD brake vans	'OO9'	Bachmann	January	
RNAD open wagons	'OO9'	Bachmann	January	
GWR 'Loriot Y' machinery truck	'OO'	Hornby	February	HM190
ZCA 'Sea Urchin' open wagons	'OO'	EFE Rail	February	HM190
BR 'Palbrick B' wagons	'OO'	KR Models	March	HM191
CDA china clay hopper wagons	'OO'	Cavalex/Trains4U/KMS	March	
VIX Ferry vans	'OO'	Rapido Trains UK	March	HM191
GWR 'Iron Mink' vans	'OO'	Rapido Trains UK	March	HM191
Class A tank wagons	'N'	Revolution Trains	April	HM192
MTV/ZKV/Zander open wagons	'N'	Revolution Trains	April	HM192
MXA 'Lobster' bogie wagons	'OO'	Bachmann	April	HM192
IIA-D Drax biomass hoppers	'N'	Revolution Trains	April	
CDA china clay hopper wagons	'O'	Kernow MRC/Dapol	May	HM193
VIX Ferry vans	'OO'	Sonic Models	May	HM193
12 ton tank wagons	'TT:120'	Hornby	May	
Seven-plank open wagons	'TT:120'	Hornby	May	
LNER/BR ventilated vans	'TT:120'	'Hornby	May	
LNER 'Toad' brake vans	'TT:120'	Hornby	May	
TUA tank wagons	'OO'	Revolution Trains/ Rainbow Railways	July	HM195
FNA-D nuclear flask carriers	'OO'	Accurascale	July	HM195
SECR six-wheel brake vans	'OO'	Rapido Trains UK	July	HM195
GWR AA20 'Toad' brake vans	'OO'	Rapido Trains UK	July	HM195
GWR four-plank open wagons	'OO'	Rapido Trains UK	July	
GWR eight-plank open wagons	'OO'	Rapido Trains UK	July	
GWR 'Loriot Y' machinery truck	'OO'	Rapido Trains UK	August	HM196
HAA MGR covered hoppers	'O'	Dapol	August	
HBA/HEA hopper wagons	'O'	Dapol	August	
GWR 12ton ventilated box vans	'O'	Dapol	August	
GWR Fruit Van A	'O'	Dapol	August	
GWR MOGO box van	'O'	Dapol	August	
SR 12ton elliptical roof vans	'O'	Dapol	August	
FNA-D nuclear flask carriers	'OO'	Revolution Trains	September	HM197
MXA 'Lobster' bogie wagons	'N'	Graham Farish	September	HM197
Newton Chambers car carriers	'OO'	Heljan	September	HM197
L&MR horse wagon	'OO'	Hornby	October	HM198
L&MR sheep wagon	'OO'	Hornby	October	HM198
SR eight-plank open wagons	'OO'	Rapido Trains UK	August	HM198
LMS five-plank open wagons	'OO'	Rapido Trains UK	October	HM198
TTA tank wagon	'O'	Dapol	October	HM198
PCA tank wagon	'O'	Dapol	October	HM198

TOTAL: 53

Hornby added a second 'P2' variant in 2023 with its streamlined, Walschaerts valve gear 2003 *Lord President*.

a Composite and a Brake Corridor Second in BR maroon to start. As with the Pullman cars, several versions were released with different running numbers and were among the first items of 'TT:120' rolling stock to appear in the train sets that arrived just before Christmas 2022. Further supplies of the vehicles on their own followed in the New Year. The Pullmans also included working table lamps and deservedly won the *Hornby Magazine* Model Railway Award for best 'TT:120' carriage or wagon.

'O' GAUGE

Two carriage projects were delivered for 'O' gauge during the year. The first appeared from Heljan with the arrival of the BR Mk 1 Covered Carriage Trucks (CCT). The all-new model features a wealth of separately fitted detailing, from handrails and lamp irons to battery boxes and handbrake levers. It also features sprung axleboxes and turned metal wheels in brass bearings, while liveries include BR lined maroon, BR unlined maroon, BR blue, Red Star parcels blue, Breakdown Train yellow, departmental olive green, Express Parcels blue and Tartan Arrow red and white for the main range releases.

Dapol's 'O' gauge range was also bolstered during the summer with the arrival of the first of its all-new London Brighton and South Coast Railway (LBSCR) Stroudley four-wheel coaches. The initial batch includes examples in LBSCR varnished mahogany with models in suburban and main line forms, modelling Brake Third, Third, Second and Composite vehicles. Further liveries are planned.

'OO9' GAUGE

Peco delivered its all-new 'OO9' Ffestiniog Railway Quarryman's coaches in late 2022, with examples finished as original Type 3 coach No.8 in red oxide, single balcony No. 6 in green and double balcony brake van No. 7 in green. Each feature neatly moulded with crisp planking, removable roofs and factory-fitted brake pipes at each end.

WAGONS

By far and away the most prolific this year, 53 wagon projects were completed across the board with an incredible selection of models produced within each project.

Leading the charge was Rapido Trains UK which delivered 11 different projects across the year starting with a selection of South Eastern and Chatham Railway (SECR) 10 ton covered vans and 12 ton ballast wagons. Complementing these were a series of distinctive SECR brake vans with verandas at each end, while a selection of single veranda versions also appeared as exclusive editions for Rails of Sheffield. Further Southern related wagons during the year included Diagram 1379 and 1400 eight-plank open wagons with 9ft and 10ft wheelbases respectively.

Great Western Modellers weren't forgotten with a series of all-new 'OO' wagons including four-plank and eight-plank opens, 'Iron Mink' box vans, an AA20 'Toad' brake van and 'Loriot Y' machinery truck. Rapido also delivered its 'OO' gauge model of the distinctive VIX Ferry Van, the first of two versions of this prototype to appear.

On the subject of the GWR 'Loriot Y' machinery truck, Hornby had delivered its version earlier in the year with models of both prototypes 41989 and 41990 being released. The model was of mainly die-cast construction and offered in GWR grey (41989) and BR grey (DW41990).

Having previously delivered its HAA merry-go-round hopper wagons in 2022, Accurascale followed this up with models of the MHA ballast open wagons in EWS and DB branded colour schemes. It also delivered its 'OO' gauge FNA-D contemporary nuclear flash carriers during the summer, which was subsequently voted best 'OO' gauge wagon in the *Hornby Magazine* Model Railway Awards. This particular wagon was another project that resulted in duplication as Revolution Trains had also previously announced its plans to produce the same wagon, which also arrived in late summer.

It was a busy year for Revolution Trains with new 'OO' releases including a selection of contemporary Ecofret container flat wagons, together with IPA car carriers which were offered in open and covered form.

Revolution Trains' specially commissioned TUA tanks also arrived in early summer, with 19 different versions available exclusively through Rainbow Railways.

Cavalex Models newly tooled HAA merry-go-round hopper wagons touched down in November 2022 with a wide selection of running numbers offered between retailers KMS Railtech and Trains4U, while the CDA china clay hopper versions followed in early 2023.

Another significant release was Bachmann's brightly coloured 'OO' MXA 'Lobster' bogie open wagon, which was one of the company's newly tooled projects revealed for that quarter's British Railway Announcements.

REVIEW OF THE YEAR

The seven-plank open wagon was an archetypical part of the steam era railway. Peco has therefore filled an important gap with its new range for the 'N' gauge market.

Bachmann's EFE Rail brand also completed a new project, with the addition of a ZCA 'Sea Urchin' engineers' spoil wagon. This model featured all-new body tooling allied to the existing SPA steel plate wagon chassis previously produced by FTG Models, Kernow Model Rail Centre and EFE Rail.

KR Models bolstered its 'OO' gauge range with the addition of all-new BR 'Palbrick B' wagons. Our review samples were full sided versions with twin openings finished in BR bauxite and offered as a triple-wagon pack. Detailing includes the screw adjusted braces to stabilise the brick loads in transit.

Finally, spanning the transition between carriages and wagons, Heljan delivered its 'OO' gauge Newton and Chambers TCV double-deck car carriers during September. Available in triple vehicle packs, as well as singly, the new car carriers are available in BR maroon with Eastern Region Car Transporter branding and in BR blue and grey Motorail guises.

'N' GAUGE

This year, seven wagon projects were completed with Revolution Trains releasing the majority. Among these are the contemporary Drax IIA-D biomass hoppers exclusively for Rails of Sheffield. Liveries cover the original scheme, together with Northern Powerhouse and Renewable Pioneers graphics.

The modern theme in 'N' continued with Revolution Trains' all-new JNA/MMA bogie box wagons, which arrived just as last year's *Hornby Magazine Yearbook* closed for press. Earlier periods weren't forgotten either, as Revolution also delivered its Class A tanks, MTV, ZKV and Zander open wagons during the year, offering further variety.

Continuing with the modern theme, Bachmann's Graham Farish range gained all-new 'N' gauge MXA 'Lobster' bogie open box wagons in September mirroring the 'OO' gauge release.

For those looking for a complete train 'off-the-shelf', Rapido Trains UK's new 'N' gauge Conflat-P container flat wagon appeared at the same time as the company's all-new 'N' gauge Class 28 Co-Bo diesel, offering a ready-to-run model of the Anglo-Scottish 'Condor' container train for the first time in the scale.

Finally for 'N' gauge, Peco released its all-new next generation seven-plank open wagons, incorporating a neatly-moulded wooden-planked body, representation of the fine metal bracing, rivet detail and handbrake levers. 14 different colour schemes formed the initial batch of releases. They proved popular with *Hornby Magazine* readers too, as they were voted best 'N' gauge wagon in the *Hornby Magazine* Model Railway Awards 2023.

'O' GAUGE

Dapol has been particularly busy on 'O' gauge projects this year developing not just its own wagons, but also exclusives for Kernow Model Rail Centre. Its all-new 'O' gauge 14 ton anchor-mounted tank wagons first appeared last October in a selection of authentic period colour schemes.

The company also delivered its 'O' gauge HEA and HBA wagons, while its popular HAA merry-go-round hopper wagons gained some additional new tooling to reflect the covered versions of these distinctive coal wagons. Steam era modellers gained several new 'O' gauge vans this year too, with the arrival of GWR 12ton ventilated vans, Fruit A box vans, MOGO vans and the SR 12ton ventilated vans with elliptical roofs.

Kernow Model Rail Centre added to its 'O' gauge portfolio with a collection of exclusive CDA china clay hopper wagons for the scale, which were rewarded with the best 'O' gauge wagon trophy in the 2023 *Hornby Magazine* Model Railway Awards. Developed by Dapol for the retailer, several liveries and running numbers were added. KMRC also produced its own 'O' gauge wagon with the arrival of a LSWR Diagram 1410 van.

Completing the 'O' gauge projects this year, Realism Redefined, the retail arm of Simon George's Britian's Biggest Model Railway, introduced its all-new 7mm scale depressed centre PCA tank wagon. Exclusive to the retailer, the model has been produced by Heljan with ten versions planned initially.

'TT:120' SCALE

Hornby's new 'TT:120' scale range launched with plans for a handful of newly tooled wagons, which arrived during the spring in the form of 12 ton tank wagons, seven-plank open wagons, LNER/BR ventilated vans and LNER 'Toad B' and 'Toad E' brake vans. The tank wagons appeared in Mobil, Carless Petrol and Fisons colour schemes, while the seven-plank wagons featured several eye-catching liveries. The vent vans appeared in LNER grey and BR bauxite, with a couple of different running numbers for each livery, while the brake vans appeared in LNER grey and BR bauxite.

This, though, is just the first tranche of planned releases from Hornby, while Peco is also developing new wagons for the fledgling scale too.

'OO9' GAUGE

Narrow gauge modelling has seen an upsurge of late, thanks in part to the increased selection of 'OO9' motive power and rolling stock. Bachmann expanded its narrow-gauge range with a selection vehicles bearing a Royal Naval Armaments Depot (RNAD) theme, including box vans, flat wagons, open wagons and brake vans. Some carried RNAD lettering while others carried preservation era liveries from the Statfold Barn Railway. Our review samples included a Mica B Meat Van with Statfold Barn SB lettering, while the flat wagon with planked ends and a sleeper load was decorated in RNAD green. Decoration to both is exemplary.

OVERALL

The past 12 months have been exceptional for railway modellers with more than 100 locomotive and rolling stock projects completed and delivered across the main scales and gauges. That is a truly phenomenal figure, and one of the highest in recent memory. We were certainly conscious of this upsurge in releases each month as we reviewed them within *Hornby Magazine*, requiring a few extra pages each month to include these new products.

However, it wasn't all plain sailing and it is unfortunate that there has been an increased level of duplication for several models, although with the increase in model railway manufacturers this is perhaps inevitable. However, this does not appear to have unduly deterred any, with more projects continuing to be announced – and we are sure there are plenty waiting in the wings to be revealed in due course. These will, of course, be covered within the pages of Hornby Magazine each month. ■

Kernow Model Centre entered the modern image 'O' gauge wagon arena with its impressive CDA china clay hoppers, developed by Dapol.

PAINTSHOP

HARDWICKE AND THE 'COMPOUND'

The high-gloss finish of locomotives working main-line steam specials is unique, but difficult to capture in model form. Using the simplest techniques imaginable, **TIM SHACKLETON** recreates the look of polished 'perfection'.

There's a view that a high-gloss finish doesn't scale down well on a ready-to-run model, but I'd disagree; it all depends on how carefully it's applied. I'm certainly less than impressed by the bland semi-matt finish applied almost universally these days, even on theoretically brand-new locomotives in pristine condition.

The colours and livery application may be exactly right, the details perfect, but this dulled finish isn't how real locomotives look at all. The limited-edition gloss-finish models from the likes of National Railway Museum collection are a significant improvement, although they don't entirely convince me either.

Recently a friend sent me photographs of 'Royal Scot' 46115 *Scots Guardsman* setting off on an enthusiasts' special. With its mirror-finish paintwork and polished brass fittings, my immediate thought was how like a 15in gauge model it looked. Only an accumulation of smuts on the tender underframe, cab roof and along the top of the boiler detracted from the showman's engine bling. Even then, it bore little resemblance to the well-groomed engines that I saw working prestigious expresses such as the 'Elizabethan' and 'Royal Scot'. Nor, from what I remember, does a museum finish much resemble the way locomotives in the heyday of steam were polished up for special workings– the 'Jones Goods' and the 'Caley Single' looked distinctly dusty to me, and certainly not fresh from a dip in the paint bath!

Until the late 1950s, however, a high-gloss finish was the default setting for most model trains – it kind of came with the territory with tinplate! It was only with the gradual

Midland Compound 1000 was used on the main line between 1959 and 1962, and again between 1975 and 1983. Here it's ready for the off with a Stephenson Locomotive Society special at Birmingham New Street in 1959. Very much the working locomotive, the superstructure is well polished but the cylinders, wheels and underframe fittings are already showing more than a hint of dustiness. **Jacy collection**

appearance of heavy freight locomotives – beginning with the excellent Hornby-Dublo '8F' 2-8-0 – that manufacturers started to feel a dull finish might be more appropriate.

Therefore, I thought I'd show you how I feel a model of a well maintained historic locomotive ought to look. Midland Compound 1000 and 'Improved Precedent' 2-4-0 No 790 *Hardwicke* are both Bachmann-NRM 'exclusives' and I wanted to present them in the condition in which – supported as always by prototype photographs – they ran in revenue service, looking not as they'd just come off shed at the start of the run, but after they'd had a chance to put a fair few miles of main line running behind them. By then some areas would still be very shiny, but others would quickly become flat and even surprisingly grubby. It is this inherent contrast that makes the treatment work.

Both engines are now stuffed-and-mounted as static exhibits and unlikely to steam again, but through modelling we at least have the opportunity to recreate as closely as possible how they'd have looked in their heyday. ■

Looking more like Gauge 1 museum-quality models that a pair of over-the-counter RTR products in 'OO' gauge, this shows just what can be done to breathe life into our locomotives without resorting to weathering techniques that are more like a branch of fine art.

Main: There's barely a fleck of dirt on either 790 or 1000 on April 24 1976, but then again, they are only about 20 miles into their run from York passing Knaresborough. It will be a different story by the time Carnforth is reached. Even so, preserved era locomotives are undoubtedly more like showman's engines than even choice railtour machines of the 1950s. **ANDREW BELL**

Right: After a brief spell on the main line in the 1970s, *Hardwicke* is once more a museum piece, though clearly well cared for by the staff at National Railway Museum, Shildon. The brake blocks are rusty but there are no oil spillages or other effects of everyday use. Only the ripples and dings in its 150-year-old fabric suggest this is the real thing, not a replica.

PAINTSHOP

STEP BY STEP: CREATING A WORKING CELEBRITY LOCOMOTIVE

▼ The range of materials I used for this project is minimal but I employ a fair old selection of brushes, each with a highly specific application! We'll look at how I used them as we come to them in turn.

The Compound's factory finish was quite flat, which made the yellow lining look gaudier. Some glint is called for! My preferred method of glossing is to apply a thin coat of Winsor & Newton's Galeria varnish using a broad flat brush – a shader. Be confident: load the brush up well and make the minimum number of passes.

When adding shine to a locomotive, use the biggest brush you can get away with but watch you don't get an unwanted build-up behind the handrails – they form an obstruction behind which you can't really paint in one continuous flowing movement. Galeria dries quickly so you only have a short time in which to brush out any surplus. See how the rich lustre of crimson lake is starting to come through.

Hardwicke's glossy finish didn't need this treatment, and the richness of LNWR 'blackberry black' was readily apparent. Unlike waterslide transfers, weathering powders don't take kindly to shiny paintwork, so I'm preparing the relevant surfaces – principally the smokebox, running plate and tender top – with a matt varnish from the Galeria range, a brand that has given me every satisfaction for many years now.

These are premium-quality models by any standards and fully deserving of the prestige of being bespoke commissions from the National Railway Museum. Tim Shackleton has made very few alterations to the as-bought models other than to enhance their life-like qualities using nothing more complicated than a few grains of weathering powder and some varnish.

PAINTSHOP

5 Once the surfaces are dry, I can start to apply weathering powders using a rounded brush called a filbert. There's no harm in using a couple of different shades of black but avoid using too many colours of weathering powder; three is quite sufficient.

6 Even on that immaculate Crimson Lake livery I wanted to add just the tiniest hint of discoloration here and there using MIG black powder applied with a filbert. Impatient as ever, I'd already done the axleboxes and tender underframe, with the effect well diffused by vigorous flicking with the same brush.

7 Smokeboxes often exhibit a bit of sparkle so as well as the expected black powder I'm brushing on a little gunmetal from the same MIG range, now available from Abteilung 502. You only need the tiniest quantities!

8 9 These before and after shots show the transformation that can be achieved with just a few dabs of powder brushed well in. All of a sudden, the underframe starts to look believable – and we've only just begun!

PAINTSHOP

STEP BY STEP — CREATING A WORKING CELEBRITY LOCOMOTIVE

10 Locomotive wheels don't stay clean for long, they quickly become coated in a film of oil from the motion, spread by centrifugal force. Over time this starts to attract brake-dust particles and track dirt. With the locomotive on its side and its paintwork (and the weathering) protected by a sheet of foam I'm brushing on small quantities of black powder. Be sure to clean the tyres afterwards.

▼ Even the fantastically detailed boiler backplate on Hardwicke can benefit from a little toning down. I've merely dabbed on black weathering powder and brushed it in well. You can see the surplus on the cab spectacles.

12 We've kept our powder dry so far… Now for the clever stuff. To start the process, I've added more than enough black powder to the top of the firebox and I'll need to blow some of it off. You can see hints of the previous application beneath this latest layer.

13 Using a specialized brush called a comb well loaded with white spirit, I'm brushing the now-diluted black powder across the firebox top and down the sides. The irregular tip of the comb helps create streaking effects.

▼ The Compound's tender rear is immaculate, showing the richness of its crimson lake livery, but I've hinted at paintwork scuffs on the footsteps by dabbing on sub-atomic grains of Gunmetal powder and brushing them well in.

14 The surfaces on real locomotives don't resemble a millpond and a few minor ripples will break up reflections and avoid the unwelcome 'mirror' effect. I'm not discouraged if, as a result of applying too much white spirit, the varnish layer starts to lift in places. Unless taken to extremes this replicates the effect of cracked, discoloured paintwork. The paint technology of the 1950s was very different.

Moulded plastic coal looks nothing like the real material, so I built up the underlying shape using coils of black plastiscene moulded by hand. I bought a big slab of the stuff and it's amazing how quickly I'm getting through it.

With both Hardwicke and the Compound, the coal supply is applied on top of the shaped mound of black plastiscene and secured with gloss varnish dribbled on with a disposable plastic pipette – another incredibly useful modelling tool.

▼ The only airbrushing on this project was the cab roof of Hardwicke. I masked the area thoroughly with recycled tape to avoid getting overspray on that beautiful lined livery. The brass fittings were coated first with masking fluid.

One of the few modifications I made to the as-delivered Compound was to replace the clumsy tender handrails with altogether finer ones made from 0.45mm nickel-silver rod. Using a No 70 bit in a pin chuck, I cautiously drilled through the beading to provide an anchor point. Drilling by hand gives you much more control than using power tools, and you can sense when the bit is about to snag.

Some extra detail was added to the front end of the 'Compound': a screw coupling from the Masokits etch, cylinder drain pipes from 0.45mm Alan Gibson brass wire, piston rods from 1mm diameter Evergreen styrene.

Key Model World MODEL

PRE-ORDER NOW! PRE-ORDER NOW! PRE-ORDER NOW!

NEW! EXCLUSIVE CAPPAGH AND VTG JNA-T WAGONS FOR 'OO'

Brand-new and available to pre-order is our exclusive collection of Revolution Trains produced Cappagh-operated JNA-T box wagons for 'OO' gauge. Eight versions are available in Royal Blue – four with Cappagh branding and four in unbranded blue with VTG logos including one version with a flashing tail lamp.

Full details are available at the Key Model World Shop.

£52.95 with tail lamp

£48.95

SCAN THE QR CODE TO VIEW OUR FULL RANGE OF EXCLUSIVE PRODUCTS ONLINE

Scan the QR code for full details of all our
www.keymodelw

SHOP

- Limited editions
- Exclusive products
- Modelling essentials

NEW! Exclusive laser-cut viaduct kits for 'OO' and 'TT:120' scales

New and exclusive to the Key Model World Shop are laser-cut kits to build this stunning model based on the Grade II listed Outwood Viaduct in Radcliffe, Manchester. The kits are available as an outer two arch kit and additional single arches to slot in between to extend the length. Full details online.

Prices: 'OO' outer two arch kit **£119.99** • 'OO' single arch kit **£47.99**
Prices: 'TT:120' outer two arch kit **£74.99** • 'TT:120' single arch kit **£29.99**

NEW! IN STOCK NOW – 'TT:120' laser-cut platform kits

Our next release for 'TT:120' scale is a pair of platform kits based on those featuring in our 'TT:120' layout build series. Option A makes a 1,115mm long, 60mm wide platform with a 156mm wide section to accommodate Hornby's Skaledale 'TT:120' station – TT9002. Option B makes a 950mm long, 60mm wide platform with a 100mm wide section to accommodate the Skaledale 'TT:120' waiting room - TT9003.

PRE-ORDER NOW! COMING IN DECEMBER – Great Northern Railway Tunnel Portals

New and available to pre-order now for delivery in December are our laser-cut kits for a double track tunnel portal based on the Great Northern Railway design at Hadley Wood. The kits are available for 'OO' and 'TT:120 scales.

Prices: 'OO' Gauge **£54.99** **Prices:** 'TT:120' **£29.99**

NEW! NEW! NEW! NEW! NEW!

WE ARE AN OFFICIAL HORNBY TT:120 STOCKIST!

Shop the full Hornby TT:120 range on the Key Model World Shop including locomotives, carriages, wagons, track and accessories as well as buildings.

modelling products or visit...
orld.com/shop

REALITY CHECK

THE FIRST AMERICAN INVASION

An alien object on the Down Slow at Hatch End, Middlesex, on the West Coast Main Line as 'S160' 2415 heaves a heavy train up the long climb to Tring Summit sometime in the summer of 1944. In August 1945, the 1943, ALCo built 2-8-0 was documented as operating from Bw Koblenz-Lützel shed in western Germany.
C.R.L. Coles/Rail Archive Stephenson.

Most of us know of the wholesale introduction into this country of American-designed locomotives in the 1990s, but fewer might be aware of a previous influx of around 1,000 during the war years. **EVAN GREEN-HUGHES** has the back story of Rapdio's forthcoming 'S160s' and Bachmann's 'USA' tanks.

REALITY CHECK

In the dark years of the early 1940s, when Britain was engaged in war with Germany and her allies, much of the country's industrial production had been turned over to manufacturing munitions, aircraft and vehicles. This was to support the conflict and shortages of ordinary supplies such as food and clothing were commonplace. This situation began to change during 1941 when the USA commenced the shipment of essentials, an arrangement that became more commonplace in December 1941 when it entered the war outright in the aftermath of Pearl Harbour.

The entry of the USA into the conflict proved to be a pivotal moment, which meant that an invasion of Nazi occupied Europe was a realtistic future possibility, but a military campaign of such size was something that would require vast resource, including rail support; something that British industry was not in a position to provide. However, military planners had all this in mind and behind the scenes work was in progress to ensure that the army would have the rail back-up that it would require.

Planners realised that there would be a need for two basic types of locomotive for use by troops. The first would be an all-purpose heavy goods type with a low axle load while the second would be a shunting locomotive with a short wheelbase that would be capable of working around sharp corners, as found in most dock systems. Both types would have to be easily constructed and use the minimum of materials and, most importantly, would need to be easy to maintain, especially at locations where there were little or no facilities.

> *"A military campaign of such size was something that would require vast resource, including rail support"*
>
> **EVAN GREEN-HUGHES**

MADE BY LIMA

There was already a locomotive in America that satisfied the first of these criteria as the US Army had an updated version of its first war 2-8-0 Baldwin-designed freight engine, eight of which had been constructed in 1941 for domestic use. These were considered satisfactory but not ideal so when, the following year, a mass order was required in anticipation of the invasion of Europe a revised version was designed by Major J.W. Marsh of the Railway Branch of the Corps of Engineers, eventually becoming known as the 'S160'.

The 'S160' was in all respects a locomotive that was designed for a short period of war service, which could then be disposed of. As a result, it had many features that enabled rapid assembly rather than a long life, including rolled rather than cast components and it had many adaptions that made it easy to service in the field. A total of 800 examples were ordered with construction undertaken by most of the country's major manufacturers, namely the American Locomotive Company (ALCo), Baldwin and Lima, with the first locomotives coming off the production line within months of the order being placed.

So many locomotives were of no use to the war effort waiting on the other side of the Atlantic and as a result the decision was taken that as many as possible should be sent to the UK, where they could be prepared for immediate dispatch to Europe when required. Completed locomotives were therefore sent in ships, four or five at a time, across the Atlantic. Most landed at Bristol Channel ports including Cardiff and Swansea, from where around half were taken to the Great Western Railway's Newport Ebbw Junction shed, which had been taken over by the US Army specially for the purpose. Examples were also docked at Glasgow and Manchester as well as east coast ports and were dealt with by ordinary railway workshops around the country.

It is thought that 840 'S160s' arrived in this country, with a further 18 lost at sea, mostly as a result of enemy action. »

Baldwin 'S160' 2339 proves its power capability with a lengthy through goods (possibly from Southampton Docks) as it eases off the 'Berks & Hants' line at Reading and onto the Down Relief of the Great Western Main Line circa 1943.
SSPL/Getty

REALITY CHECK

Reading again, probably on the same day as the adjacent picture, sees ALCo-built 2131 paused alongside a begrimed Chruchward 'Star' 4-6-0. **SSPL/Getty**

A string of 'S100s' await anglicising at Eastleigh Works, including ex-War Department 1971 second from front...
Colour Rail

FAR AND WIDE

Once in the UK, the locomotives were prepared for service, the coupling rods that had been shipped in the tenders were fitted and each engine was steamed and subject to a road test. Those dealt with at Ebbw Junction undertook trials on the GWR, usually on a local goods working while others were merely commissioned on any suitable diagram. However, with so many new goods engines in the country and the railways being in a dire state agreement was soon reached for a number of these American-built engines to be transferred on a temporary basis to home railway companies for use on domestic goods duties. In all, 403 'S160s' were loaned out, with the GWR being the first beneficiary, which eventually rostered 174 in service. The first of these, 1604, was officially handed over in a ceremony at Paddington station on December 11 1942 where it was seen with the flags of both the USA and the UK attached to the smokebox door. Early examples went to sheds such as Banbury, but full details of their allocation were never recoded and are still difficult to track down owing to wartime information constraints.

It is known that the London Midland & Scottish Railway (LMS) took 50 locomotives while the Southern Railway had only six and the War Department itself had five for use on home railways. However, the biggest user in the UK was the London and North Eastern (LNER) which took 168, but which also recommissioned and ran-in a further 38, which then went elsewhere. These were concentrated at six main sheds and worked heavy goods trains particularly on the east coast mainline between Newcastle and Edinburgh, the Great Central line south of Annesley and the Great Eastern around March.

By August 1943, it was being reported to the Government that sufficient locomotives were on hand to satisfy the immediate needs of the home railways and from that point on the emphasis shifted from loaning out new arrivals to finding somewhere to store them. Three sites were selected in South Wales, at Cadoxton, Penrhos and Treherbert, which in time held 355 of the 2-8-0s, all of which had completed commissioning and running-in trials, but which had their cabs boarded-up as a temporary measure.

GOOD AND BAD

The use of the 'S160s' in Britain was not without its problems. All of the locomotives had to have their tyres re-profiled to the UK standard and yet, even so, they were prone to derailment, particularly when running tender first. A major issue was the design of the firebox where the stays tended to overheat and then fail owing to metal fatigue. This could also be exacerbated by any build-up of scale on the firebox. The class was also fitted with only one boiler water gauge which was of an American design unfamiliar to most British crews and which could be rendered useless by inadvertent use of a cut-off valve, which was positioned in such a way that it was often mistaken for something else. This meant that enginemen could be misled as to the actual level of water in the boiler. The locomotives also suffered from inadequate lubrication of the axles, which often led to overheating.

Unfortunately, the deficiencies in the design of the firebox, coupled with the water gauge arrangement led to a number of accidents, of which there were three within ten months. The first of these led to the death of a GWR fireman when the firebox of 2403 collapsed in November 1943, the second involving 2363 occurred as it was hauling a goods train between Ipswich and Whitemoor, with the driver sustaining a broken leg and the fireman burns in the subsequent explosion and the third being within South Harrow tunnel when 1707 exploded while hauling a goods train from Neasden to Woodford.

Nevertheless, they were regarded as very competent engines, and many of their features such as self-cleaning smokeboxes, rocker ashpans and drop grates were subsequently adopted in this country.

With arrangements for the invasion of Europe in full swing, the War Department recalled all the loan engines during 1944, which by all accounts caught the railways off-guard and resulted in a rush to get the locomotives ready for shipment to Europe. Many needed Works attention and so it was

> *It was being reported to the Government that sufficient locomotives were on hand to satisfy the immediate needs of the home railways*

EVAN GREEN-HUGHES

some time before all were available. Naturally, those that were stored were removed first with the bulk of these engines leaving the sidings in late August and early September 1944. Most of these were taken to Southampton and disembarked in Cherbourg in France. In addition, around another 70 were landed directly from America and were then towed across the UK to be transferred to France without further preparation.

Despite the 'S160s' widespread use all over the country, by the end of 1944 all had been withdrawn from domestic service and deployed all over Europe. Many remained in service for many years thereafter. None were brought back for service in Britain, but six have subsequently been reimported from other countries for use on heritage lines. Some of these have provided appropriate North American motive power for the seasonal, family-oriented 'Polar Express' trains.

ENTER THE 'YANK TANK'

Although less numerous than the 'S160s', the other main American import of the period was destined to have a much longer service life in the UK. This was the 'S100' 0-6-0 tank engine, designed by Colonel Howard Hill in 1942 for heavy shunting and short-trip goods duties. Around 400 of these were built and the majority of these shipped across to the UK. Unlike their big sisters, these engines were merely placed in store, with the majority going initially to Barry Junction, where they were conveniently situated for the Ebbw Junction maintenance facility.

The 'S100' was a rugged, short-wheelbase, no-frills engine with outside cylinders and valve gear, cast steel bar frames, and no running plates. Examples were built by three of the USA's major manufacturers: Porter, Davenport and Vulcan between 1942 and 1944. Delivery was to a number of locations from which the engines were towed dead to nearby sheds for the coupling rods and other fittings to be attached, prior to being placed in store. However, some were temporarily 'borrowed' by those depots for shunting and a small number were also temporarily loaned to Welsh collieries. As the war progressed, most were dispatched to Europe, with many leaving from Newport Docks, but it is thought that fewer than half actually left for Europe, with the remainder regrouped and put back into store. Around 42 of these were taken to Newbury Racecourse station where they remained, even after hostilities ended.

In a remarkable twist, the stored engines came to the attention of Oliver Bulleid, Chief Mechanical Engineer of the Southern Railway, who was seeking replacements for the aging 'B4' 0-4-0Ts that were used in Southampton Docks. The War Department offered either the American tanks or the British Hunslet 'J94' design, but Bulleid preferred the 'S100s' because of their shorter wheelbase and outside valve gear. As a result, 4326 was taken to Eastleigh Works before being experimentally deployed at the docks, where it proved to be a success.

EASTLEIGH TWEAKS

Following this, it and 14 others were purchased for the princely sum of £2,500 each, towed in batches from Newbury to Eastleigh. There it was discovered that there were some differences between Porter and Vulcan-built engines, as a result of which there was an exchange of five Porter engines for Vulcan examples. This left the Southern with one Porter engine as there were no more Vulcans available. As a result, it was agreed to take an extra Porter locomotive to provide spares for the first one. »

In a remarkable twist, the stored engines came to the attention of Oliver Bulleid, Chief Mechanical Engineer of the Southern Railway

EVAN GREEN-HUGHES

... and this is the result. That very locomotive now sports Southern Railway Bulleid livery, with modified bunker and cab.
W. Croughton/Rail Archive Stephenson

The sole Porta-built (1942) 'USA' tank to enter Southern service was USATC 1264, later DS 233, shuffles wagons in the shadow of the Southampton Ocean Liner Terminal on June 6 1964.
Colour Rail

Turned out in British Railways lined green, 30064 powers away from Baynards on the Woking – Guildford leg of the RCTS 'Midhurst Belle' railtour on October 18 1964. Withdrawn at the end of Southern Region steam in July 1967, the engine found sanctuary at the Bluebell Railway before passing into private ownership in 2022.
Colour Rail

Steam heat equipment was added at Eastleigh, as were vacuum ejectors, Ashford pattern injectors and sliding windows to the cabs. Because of the time taken to do all these modifications, it was to be November 1947 before all were at employed at work in the docks. Following operational experience, cab roof ventilators were added, as were British-style regulators and extended coal bunkers.

The American engines were numbered 61-74 by the Southern and later passed to British Railways where they became 30061-074. They spent almost all of their working lives in the docks except for a brief period in 1955 when 30061/066 were loaned to the Midland Region, one being used in Liverpool and the other in Kentish Town. Both were, however, back within a month, although 30061 was again on its travels the next year when it spent a short time at Cricklewood.

In 1962 the USA tanks were replaced by new Ruston diesel shunters and as a result two went to Redbridge sleeper depot, two to Lancing Carriage works and one each to Meldon Quarry and to Ashford Wagon works.

By 1967 all were out of service, but fate lent a hand to 30065/070 which ran hot while being towed from Ashford for scrap, being dumped at Tonbridge from where they were rescued for preservation by the Kent and East Sussex Railway and removed by road. 30068 ended up at Betteshanger colliery in Kent after a period supplying steam to dry-docked ships from where it was eventually condemned. 30064 ended up at the Bluebell Railway while 30072 was purchased for the Keighley & Worth Valley Railway where it was to be one of the first engines to work there in the preservation era. Also of interest is that more locomotives to the same design were later built in Eastern Europe after the war with two finding their way to this country where they have received the fictitious BR identities 30075-076.

Many more remain around the globe. Both the 'S160s' and 'S100s' lasted for a great deal of time in Europe and further afield, and did much to put war-damaged railways back on track after the hostilities ended.

Today we can enjoy a number of our heritage railways as a fitting reminder of the times when American engines 'invaded' our country for the first time. ■

THE ELUSIVE USTAC DIESEL

Although not generally known, there was a third type of American-built locomotive that was imported into the UK during the war: the USATC centre cab Bo-Bo diesel. Three versions are reported to have been seen in the UK; the majority likely to have been '65 tonners' built by the Whitcomb Locomotive Company.

Little is known of their time here although they are reported to have been reactivated at Ebbw Vale and then run-in on nearby GWR metals. Apparently, such running-in trials were hampered by the company's inability to provide suitable crews with diesel experience, a single driver who signed diesel railcars was all that could be offered at that time!

Around 65 such diesels were in the country at their highest point and there are reports of them being operated at Eastleigh and Southampton, but whether this was in connection with their embarkation for France is not known. All of the diesels were shipped to Europe in 1944 where they performed admirably, particularly when later transferred to the Middle East.

After the war in Europe ended some were taken back to America and then refurbished for further use in the war against Japan.

Owing to the secrecy surrounding railway operations during the war years there are few photographs of the American locomotives at work, compared with the quantity taken during peace time, but these engines did contribute a considerable amount to the war effort, even if much of it was in secrecy.

FLYING SCOTSMAN IN THE 21ST CENTURY

Hornby's well-regarded Gresley A3 Pacific is an ideal basis for super detailing, so **RICHARD HALL** models the three unique conditions worn by *Flying Scotsman* since 2000.

A name that needs little introduction, *Flying Scotsman* lays claim to be the world's most famous steam locomotive, with high-profile exploits in main line service and an infamously varied preserved life.

Constructed in 1923 as a Nigel Gresley-deign LNER A1 class as 1472, the later branded 4472 *Flying Scotsman* achieved notoriety for hauling the first non-stop run from London to Edinburgh in 1928 and the first accredited 100mph record in 1934. Withdrawn by British Railways in 1963, the A3 (as it was classed by then) began a unique four-decade preservation career, including visits to North America and Australia under the care of three successive custodians.

Purchased by the National Railway Museum in 2004, *Flying Scotsman* was eventually outshopped again in 2016 after a protracted overhaul and reached its centenary in 2023. The Pacific has arguably gained an even higher profile over the last eight years of running UK main and heritage lines and marking the history of this exceptional locomotive in miniature seemed appropriate.

Hornby's A3 tooling from 2005 still holds its own, but any example can still benefit from further detailing: ranging from the straightforward addition of painted details, etched nameplates and lamps, through to assembling more advanced etched brass

A range of scratch built and kit details combined to both improve Hornby's A3 and make each model specifically tailored to the three guises of *Flying Scotsman* between 2005 and 2019. From left to right, early-2016 interim NE black 502/103/60103, 2019-era 60103 and 2005-era 4472.

components and scratch building. The aim for this project was replicating the three principal guises carried between 2000 and 2019, which also meant including the surprisingly high number of preservation-era details belonging to the locomotive.

Firstly, Hornby's R2441 was used to replicate 4472 in the rather tired 2005 NRM condition that your writer first remembers it in, complete with smokebox mounted chime whistle and 'deflectors (the latter temporarily removed that summer). As this model of 4472 is purely for mainline use, a fixed LED high intensity headlight was installed, using a ModelU tail lamp suitably drilled out to contain a warm white Nano LED.

Hornby's R3100 replicates the striking NE black livery worn on *Flying Scotsman*'s »

Prototype photographs are vital to inform modelling and this view even shows the unique white 'quartering' that featured on the centre driving wheel of *Flying Scotsman*. Its influence on encouraging new and young people into the hobby is also clear, with the author and his father standing in front of 4472 at Didcot in 2005.

WORKBENCH

King's Cross' famous barrelled roof greets *Flying Scotsman* in November 2022, just as it has done countless times for 100 years. **NICK BRODRICK**

premature unveiling in 2011. This donor is a good basis for becoming the hybrid NE/BR black undercoat carried by 60103 on its main line trial runs and at the East Lancashire Railway in early 2016. The excellent Brassmasters A3 detailing kit supplied the smoke deflectors required for this model; a challenge to shape but a definite improvement for any A3 fitted with these distinctive German-style 'blinkers'.

The third model replicates 60103 as running in 2019 and uses the R3443 '2016 Rededication' edition of 60103. Outwardly, this loco does not appear significantly changed. However, like the 2005 condition 4472, this *Flying Scotsman* has been upgraded with the comprehensive Brassmasters detailing kit and numerous scratch-built parts. Full cab, tender and innumerable 0.3mm pipework detail not present on proprietary models has also been added, but for sanity this might be a step too far for most to even want to replicate!

While the soldered brass detailing, significant tender modifications and miniscule lubricator pipe runs all required more advanced skills, eyesight and patience, the end result has created three unique (and excessively) accurate models of *Flying Scotsman*. Carrying out duplicates of a project simultaneously can enable more efficient modelling time, and yet with over 100 hours of modelling across the three Pacifics, deciding on just one era of *Flying Scotsman* to replicate might prove to be a wise choice!

A locomotive that has encouraged many to gain an interest in railways, hopefully these three models show just how unique this celebrity locomotive really is. ■

EXCLUSIVE ONLINE FEATURE!

Visit our website – *www.keymodelworld.com* – to see an online guide to detailing Hornby's A3 into three different versions of *Flying Scotsman*.

WHAT WE USED		
PRODUCT	SUPPLIER	CAT NO.
4472/60103 etched name plates	www.fox-transfers.co.uk	FEP60103
Flying Scotsman record plaques	www.fox-transfers.co.uk	FEP4472ACPO
LNER A3 Class wheel lining	www.fox-transfers.co.uk	FRH4534/10B
'The Flying Scotsman' etched headboard	www.fox-transfers.co.uk	FEPHB301/2
1990s/2000s electrification flashes	www.railtec-models.co.uk	4mm-1058
Detailing kit for Hornby A3	www.brassmasters.co.uk	H210
Short handrail knobs	www.alangibsonworkshop.com	4M53
12.5mm 10 spoke bogie wheels	www.markits.com	A2_00BR.5BS
LNER/BR(E) headlamps	www.modelu3d.co.uk	2060
BR Battery Tail Lamp Mk2	www.modelu3d.co.uk	2081
JE Detailing 'Britannia' chime whistle	www.phoenix-paints.co.uk	4-10105
Plasticard sheet – various thicknesses	www.slatersplasticard.com	Various
Plasticard rod sections	www.slatersplasticard.com	Various
Acrylic paints and weathering powders	www.humbrol.com	Various
Phoenix Precision enamel paints	www.phoenix-paints.co.uk	See text
Railmatch Acrylic paints and varnishes	www.howesmodels.co.uk	Various
Railmatch Enamel satin varnish	www.howesmodels.co.uk	1408
Tamiya black panel line accent colour	www.amazon.co.uk	87131
99.8% Isopropyl Alcohol	www.amazon.co.uk	
0.4mm flexible blackened copper wire	www.amazon.co.uk	
0.5mm brass rod	www.albionalloys.com	BR1
1.0mm brass rod	www.albionalloys.com	BW10
Locomotive Staff	www.bachmann.co.uk	36-047
6mm Tamiya masking tape	www.tamiya.com	87030
Decoder wire (32 Gauge)	www.dccconcepts.com	DCW-32SET
Firebox flicker kit	www.roads-and-rails.com	
Daylight white nano LED	www.dccconcepts.com	LED-NLSW
Dapol class 68 air pipes	www.dccsupplies.com	112200
Scale screw link couplings	www.hornby.com	R7200
Zimo 8-pin MTC DCC Decoder	www.agrmodelrailwaystore.co.uk	MX600R

STEP BY STEP: 21ST CENTURY *FLYING SCOTSMANS*

SKILL LEVEL: Intermediate

1. The detailing undertaken on the 2005-condition 4472 was the most involved of the three and it is worth noting the differences Hornby has tooled in this condition from the factory. The rear model is the 2011 release (R3336) that was made assuming that *Flying Scotsman* would regain LNER apple green after overhaul with its current A3 boiler. Whereas the front model is the correct donor to use and dates from 2005 (R2441); commendably, it features an A4 boiler, with uniquely spaced washout plugs, that were present until overhaul in 2006.

2. With the unmodified 1928 corridor tender (rear), this first stage is to cut down the upper raves on the water filler area of the tender (middle). This applicable to any preservation-era model of *Flying Scotsman* as its tender was modified during the 1948 exchange trials. Next, the water scoop return housing was removed (front) and the upper continuation of the coal space was installed using 1mm Plasticard, with chamfered edges to minimise filling required.

3. Hornby's LNER Pacific tenders all feature tender interior mouldings that clip into the outer tender shell, meaning that modifications are made simpler with these inserts removed. From observing photographs, I realised that I had cut too much of the raves away and this error was corrected by squaring off the cut out and carefully forming 0.5mm Plasticard to the correct shape. At the same time, the corridor tender tunnel was raised and sanded flush to the new upper streamlining.

4. The cab face of the tender required several additions to all three 'Scotsmans, with the 2005 variant being the most straightforward; only requiring a single tool box, this was scratch built from Plastruct styrene sheet and U channel section and still features on the locomotive to this day, housing the GSM-R (Global System for Mobile Communications-Railway) equipment. Also visible are the two small cylinders and pipework mounted to the top of the coal area in the tender, again scratch built using 3.2mm diameter Plastruct rod and 0.3mm brass wire.

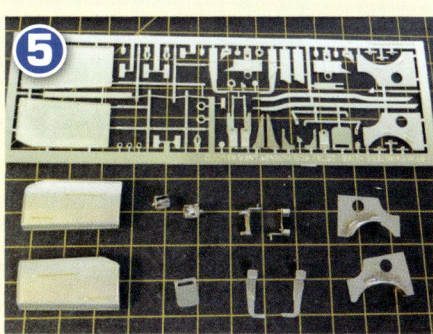

5. The Brassmasters detailing etch is an ideal kit to upgrade any A3. Many of the parts are small and require carful folding, making the purchase of photoetch cutters and a folding tool essential. The small buffer housings are a unique detail not often modelled but do require a steady hand to solder together. The steps and frame covers are also significant upgrades but will restrict the minimum curve radius that the model can negotiate.

6. In order to model the hybrid NE black carried in 2016, the German-style smoke deflectors included in the Brassmasters kit were ideal and also make for a big improvement over the thicker plastic 'deflectors supplied by Hornby. Careful use of a blade edge and photoetch bending tool evenly formed the subtle curve and angled lower edge required, before the inner frame can then be folded, similarly shaped and soldered into position.

7. Plastic cylinder drain cocks supplied with many proprietary models are well detailed and offer a degree of flexibility for negotiating tighter trackwork, however, if track curvature allows, adding brass cylinder drain cocks is a good upgrade to consider. Simple to scratch build, three sections of 0.4mm brass wire were carefully shaped and soldered together to form a strong bond. Scratch building these details also meant that the 'long' LNER type carried in 2005 and 'short' BR-era drains currently fitted could be accurately modelled.

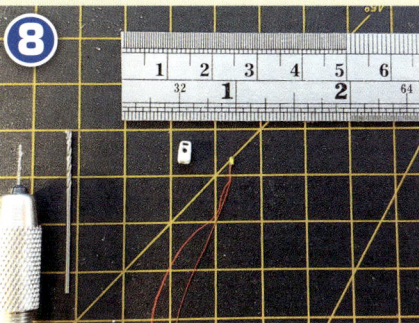

8. Between 1999 and 2005, *Flying Scotsman* was predominantly a main line locomotive due to the removal of vacuum brakes and fitment of air braking, this made adding the necessary main line high intensity headlight an interesting feature. The ModelU end of train light is 3D printed, making it automatically insulated and easy to drill out for an LED, unlike using a Whitemetal component. DCC Concepts pre-wired daylight white Nano LEDs are an ideal size for lamps and are supplied pre-wired on easily hidden enamelled wire.

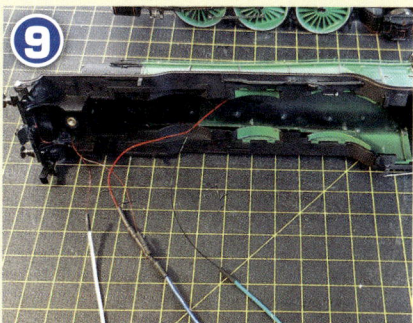

9. As the LNER liveried 4472 was one of the original releases of Hornby A3 with the 8-pin DCC decoder mounted in the locomotive, this makes adding further lighting simpler than needing to route multiple wires back to the tender. Installing an orange firebox glow further enhances a model and a kit produced by Roads and Rails was easily fitted once the firehole door was opened out with a pin vice and scalpel. As per NMRA wiring colours, blue is the function common positive going to both front and firebox LEDs, while each was allocated as F0 and F1 respectively.

WORKBENCH

Three *Flying Scotsmans*... three very different variants.

Etched buffer housings and footsteps, replacement wire draincocks and 3D-printed bardic lamp are just some of the details Richard Hall has incorporated on his 2016-era model of *Flying Scotsman*.

Hornby's model doesn't come with a cab roof sheet, so Richard has made his own from crumped paper.

STEP BY STEP: 21ST CENTURY *FLYING SCOTSMANS*

10 The undercoat finish worn in early 2016 was unique, with the smokebox, wheels and cab interior all featuring gloss top-coat paint for BR green, while the boiler, splashers and tender were heavily contrasted in matt dark grey. Humbrol black weathering powder achieves a flat matt finish, followed by a dark grey wash of Railmatch roof dirt and black and finished with a matt varnish to protect the finish, seal the weathering powders and flatten the paint further.

11 *Flying Scotsman* has carried a flush-finished smokebox door in recent years, meaning that the prominent rivets on the door and hinge straps on all three models needed cautious paring away with a fresh scalpel blade and 1000 grit sanding sticks. The black NE model additionally needed BR number and shed plates adding (carefully painted Fox products) and also a lowered top lamp bracket and split handrail (Silver Tay and Alan Gibson respectively). The model only features the standard detailing.

12 In a sharp contrast to the matt black worn by the locomotive in 2016, *Flying Scotsman* in 2005 featured a signature 'oily rag' finish. As shown on the third model of 60103, this can be achieved by adding layers of varnish, however I used white spirit and cotton buds to physically polish 4472. Using this technique also only targets where a cleaner would regularly reach and leaves a good surface for weathering washes later, but be sure to be in a well-ventilated room while using white spirit.

13 A further detail unique to 4472 in the early-2000s was the chime whistle positioned on the smokebox and this was all the more important to include as I made the smoke deflectors on this model removable, reflecting the change briefly made to real locomotive in summer 2005. The chime whistle comes from the JE castings range and looks prototypically substantial, while the pipework was formed from 0.33 and 0.45mm brass wire. Also note the prominent smokebox and hinge rivets before removal.

14
As etched parts, the Brassmasters details are durable and make a huge visual improvement to both 4472 and 60103. The steps fitted by Hornby are inaccurate as one-piece mouldings attached to the curved running plate, whereas the Brassmasters kit allows the correct mounting under the buffer housings. All brass components were etch metal primed and top coat black painted before installation and the steps, buffers and frame extensions were all soldered to each other in situ for the best alignment.

15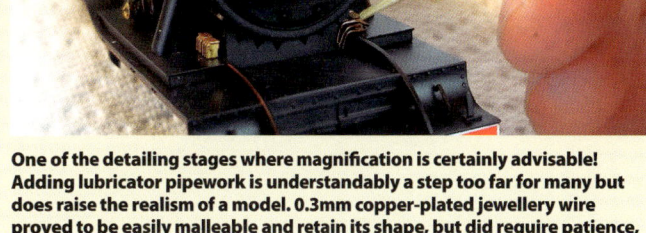
One of the detailing stages where magnification is certainly advisable! Adding lubricator pipework is understandably a step too far for many but does raise the realism of a model. 0.3mm copper-plated jewellery wire proved to be easily malleable and retain its shape, but did require patience, trial and error to form each curve on such short sections of wire. Pipework was also added only where easily visible, including for the running plate lubricators and set pipes wrapping around the lower corners of the firebox.

16
There are a number of upgrades to steam locomotive bogie wheels that can be carried out and Hornby's wheels as-supplied (right) can be significantly improved by evenly sanding the edge of the metal tyre flat with the plastic centre, therefore removing the join between the two. Full replacement wheels, from the likes of Markits and Alan Gibson (centre and left), offer a far more refined all-metal design, with flat tyre faces and finer flange profiles.

17
In order to remove the bare metal tyre edge on the LNER green wheelsets on 4472, re-lining offered the neatest solution and was not a difficult process. To remove the bare metal edge around all of the wheels, a black permanent marker is suitable as it will not chip away on such a vulnerable area. The bogie and driving wheels were then all re-lined using a pack from Fox Transfers, carefully positioned with cocktail sticks and excess water removed with cotton buds.

STEP BY STEP: 21ST CENTURY *FLYING SCOTSMANS*

The bright shine of coupling rods fitted to many ready-to-run locomotives can be substantially improved by painting valve gear to an oily shine and darker burnished appearance. After cleaning the rods of any oil residue with Isopropyl alcohol, a mix of Humbrol Satin black (85), Aluminium (56) and Railmatch 'Oily Steel' (2415) was applied in two coats to give a polished look for 60103, but the colour can be changed and darkened with higher quantities of black and oily steel to suit any prototype.

The weathering on the interiors of tenders can be remarkably varied and intricate, however as these tenders would have coal loads fitted, an effective grimy dark brown was applied. Mixing black acrylic with Railmatch frame dirt (2402) gave the base shade and was brush painted in two coats, with the second using a stippling technique to replicate the rough texture of the metal in the coal space. Lighter browns were then dry brushed around water filler are to indicate fresh rust.

While aspects of *Flying Scotsman* in 2005 were certainly looking tired, as in many cases of preserved locomotives, less is more with weathering. Underframe details, such as tender wheels, brake rigging and frames are all rarely cleaned in reality and are brush-painted with varying shades of Railmatch roof dirt, frame dirt and black. In order to not totally obscure the fine red LNER lining on 4472s, matt black was dry brushed over the frames.

Replicating engrained grime along boiler bands, pipework and behind handrails brings more depth to the finish of a model and works particularly well alongside an otherwise polished finish. A black wash or Tamiya panel line accent is ideal to highlight difficult to clean areas of a locomotive that would naturally build up dirt. A thinned dark grey wash was similarly applied across the boiler and cabsides, with most removed by white spirit-soaked cotton buds.

22 An important upgrade for any A3 comes in the form of etched name and works plates from the comprehensive Fox range, in addition to a pair of suitable headboards. With the NE black *Flying Scotsman* not requiring any nameplates, the Fox etched BR smokebox numberplate was used and care was taken to use the curled font '6' that is accurate for 60103. For the 2005-era 4472, etched Australian distance record plaques were also effective and adding full relief to the centre splashers.

23 The end result of concentrated detailing and weathering on 4472, complete with accurate spaced white tyre marks on the centre driving wheel. Pipework was only added where visible, with all variants of *Flying Scotsman* featuring 0.3mm pipes running along the edges of both running plates. This view also shows the difference made by using weathering washes and a polished finish to create an accurate 'oily rag' effect without the need for varnishes or an airbrush.

24 A final imposing view of the 2005-era locomotive, complete with working headlight, firebox glow and prominent chime whistle. Removable smoke deflectors are a unique feature to add and use two short sections of 0.33mm brass wire, glued onto the smoke deflector mounting pins, that simply slot into two small holes in the smokebox.

No main line registered steam locomotive would be complete without its support coach. The National Railway Museum's Mark 1 BSK 99953 (Bachmann) is an authentic match for 4472 from 2004 onwards.

Alec Pearce & Vernon Crump have 'broken down' with their lorry! No problem for Driver Sam Weech and Fireman Dan Taylor who would clatter it out of the way, only to then be challenged to a duel with Hawkins' steam roller.
Mary Evans/Studiocanal Films Ltd/Alamy

CHANGE FOR TITFIELD!

Ealing Comedy *The Titfield Thunderbolt* must rank as the most modelled railway film set. **HORNBY MAGAZINE** reflects on why it is so well loved and the ranges of ready-to-run models it has inspired.

Colour photographs of *Lion* dressed in full Titfield Thunderbolt garb are rare. This is a still from the film showing the short-lived livery and the vintage carriage body prop mounted on a 'Loriot Y' well wagon.
Pictorial Press Ltd/Alamy

CHANGE FOR TITFIELD!

By the 1950s, Monkton Combe station hadn't seen a passenger train for a quarter of a century. Boarded-up in 1925, this quaint byway nestled in the north Somerset hills, three miles from Bath, had been shut for more years than it had been open. Even as its unlikely existence eked beyond the Camerton branch's final closure as a goods-only line in February 1951, its slide toward irreversible decay seemed inevitable.

That was until the following year when the Ealing Studios circus rolled into the sleepy village.

Not only did Director Charles Crichton bring an army of actors, camera and production crew to Monkton Combe, he added restored 1838-built Liverpool & Manchester Railway (MR) 0-4-2 57 *Lion* and a Wisbech & Upwell Tramway (Great Eastern Railway built) car as key props for what became one the studio's best-loved comedy films, *The Titfield Thunderbolt*.

Suddenly, Monkton Combe was a hive of activity, populated by some of Britain's most recognisable actors including Sid James and Stanley Holloway.

This is the story of how the population of Monkton Combe, dressed as the fictional village of Titfield fought – and won – a battle to overturn the Ministry of Transport's decision shut its branch line. That was in the face of fierce competition from villains Pearce & Crump (played by Ewan Roberts and Jack MacGowran), who had tried to establish a private bus service to another fantasy town: Mallingford.

The Titfield – Mallingford line's two featured trains were, of course, the stuff of prototype fantasy. The first, formed of '14XX' 1401, Wisbech tramcar, cattle van and 'Toad' brakevan; and the second, revival train with *Lion* (running as *Thunderbolt*), a freelance four-wheel carriage body mounted on a 'Lowmac' and 'Toad'. All the same, these unusual ensembles still epitomised the typical, bucolic branch line situation familiar to thousands in the pre-1955 Modernisation Plan era.

Indeed, the subject matter was representative of an era of significant railway events. The reopening of the world's first preserved railway, the 2ft 3in gauge Talyllyn, in May 1951 had provided the inspiration for script writer T. E. B. 'Tibby' Clarke. That extended as far as anecdotal tales of locomotives with empty water tanks having to be topped up using buckets filled from a nearby stream, and passengers being asked to get off another stranded train to give it a push!

The *Titfield Thunderbolt* was also a portent for the axe that Dr Beeching would later brandish over hundreds of branch lines following the publishing of his infamous *Reshaping of British Railways* report of 1963 – and the many battles fought by local populations to save 'their' railway.

BRIBES AND BULLETS
The tone of *The Titfield Thunderbolt* is established in the very first sequence as Southern Region air-smoothed 'West Country' No. 34043 *Combe Martin* hurries south »

The ostensibly disused Monkton Combe station is probably the busiest it has ever been in the summer of 1952 as Ealing Studios' production crew swarms around former Wisbech & Upwell tramcar 7. Mary Evans/Studiocanal Films Ltd/Alamy

across the Somerset & Dorset Joint line's Midford viaduct, just as '14XX' 1401 dives beneath it on the grass-infested Camerton branch.

These run-pasts took several attempts to correctly time, demonstrating the cooperation that Ealing Studios enjoyed with British Railways which had lent Ealing several of its locations, locomotives and crews.

A Thomas-and-Bertie-esque race then ensues between the branch line train and Pearce & Crump's new Bedford OB.

The train wins, but the victory is short-lived. What follows are several subsequent acts of underhand sabotage by the road transport entrepreneurs: namely draining a GWR water crane by peppering it with rifle bullets; bribing Harry Hawkins (Sid James) to duel his Aveling & Porter steam roller with 1401 on a level crossing; and then ultimately wrecking the '14XX' and its tramcar (by now converted to a buffet for seasoned drinker and railway revival financier Walter Valentine, played by Stanley Holloway) in the dead of night by freewheeling it across a broken rail and down an embankment.

The Collett 0-4-2T was supported by a stunt double for some of the filming; 1456, although renumbered as 1401 for continuity. It is important to note, however, that the crash scene was represented using models and no tank engines were harmed in the making of this film!

Another '14XX' appears later that night. Dan Taylor (Hugh Griffith), 1401's now former fireman, and Mr Valentine drunkenly hijack '14XX' 1462 from Mallingford shed with the intention of saving the Titfield service.

Instead, the bleary-eyed duo misalign the turntable (filmed at Oxford shed) and inadvertently drive the GWR tank engine down the streets of Mallingford (played by a full-size dummy locomotive!) and wrecking a second '14XX' of the night; this time into a sizeable oak tree.

With under two days until the do-or-die inspection train for the Ministry of Transport

The milk dock at Bristol Temple Meads is the unlikely setting for an ancient Liverpool & Manchester 0-4-2T as it takes on the façade of Mallingford at the moment of *Lion's* grand finale triumph.
Mary Evans/Studiocanal Films Ltd/Alamy

was due to run, logic suggests that the train crashes and arrests of its chief backer and only fireman would have been the final nail in the coffin for Titfield's 'save our railway' campaign.

LION ROARS AGAIN

But as befits any good plot twist, Titfield's central character, Reverend, and nominated steam driver, Sam Weech (George Relph), suddenly hits upon the seemingly wacky idea to extract the historic 0-4-2 *Thunderbolt* from Titfield Museum and then steam it to haul the train. He even enlists visiting enthusiast friend Ollie Matthews, the Bishop of Wilchester, to fire it vice Dan Taylor.

Many hands made its hair-raising extraction down the soaring museum steps possible. The cumbersome sequence was again filmed using a full-size wooden dummy locomotive.

However, it was the real-deal *Lion* that was coupled, by rope, to the 'Loriot Y' well wagon (comically mounted with Dan's re-purposed and borrowed 'grounded carriage body' home) for what have become some of the most loved, if not famous, railway sequences of the Fifties.

Lion had been first reactivated by the London, Midland & Scottish Railway for the centenary celebrations of the LMR in 1930, having not previously run for 73 years.

> "The Titfield Thunderbolt *was also a portent for the axe that Dr Beeching would later brandish over hundreds of branch lines*"

The complete Titfield – Mallingford reopening train is available in two different train packs. Rapido

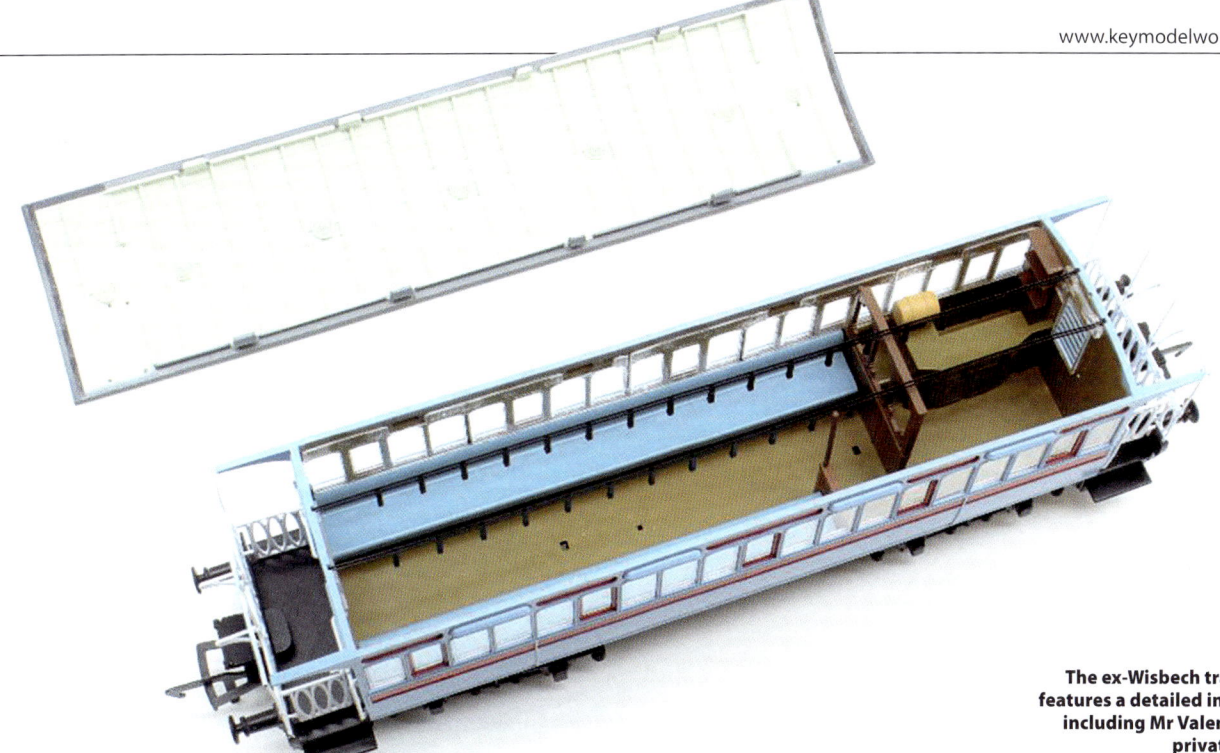

The ex-Wisbech tramcar features a detailed interior including Mr Valentine's private bar.
Rapdio

Its subsequent, if infrequent, film roles made it the logical, if not only, choice to represent a suitably archaic looking machine embodying the Titfield & Mallingford Railway's pioneering locomotive.

Unlike previous on-screen appearances, The Titfield Thunderbolt would be its first in glorious Technicolour. To make it stand out, the much of the black painted areas were replaced with red, plus decorative gold chevrons on the chimney. Gaudy, yes. Memorable, certainly.

By any standards, the concluding scene of Thunderbolt arriving at Mallingford, is remarkable. That's because its final destination is actually Bristol Temple Meads, bustling with Top Link Western Region motive power.

Witnessing Lion, alias Thunderbolt, an 1838-era antique looking really quite lost amid the number of four-cylinder, superheated 100-mph capable 'Star' and 'Castle' 4-6-0s remains just as bizarre to modern eyes as it must have to viewers in 1953.

Yet, this mix of fantasy and reality was undoubtedly a clinching factor in what made The Titfield Thunderbolt a film for the ages.

And the ending was, of course, a happy one. The enterprising villagers earned the approval of the Ministry of Transport to a chorus of cheers and whistles.

TINY TITFIELD... MINIATURE MALLINGFORD

The fact that the Ealing comedy remains so popular is why contemporary model manufacturers have taken the plunge into making 'OO' examples of various pieces from the film.

This year, Rapido Trains UK revealed its own, Studio Canal licenced, Thunderbolt range.

There is striking rendition of the revival inspection train: Thunderbolt, 'Loriot Y' 41989 with the fictitious carriage body (complete with fully detailed interior furnishings) and GWR Diagram AA20 'Toad' brakevan W68740.

With Hattons having only relatively recently produced a 'OO' gauge '14XX', it is understandable why Rapido have (so far) opted not to follow suit. Yet, it has still invested in a new tooling of the buffet car; Great Eastern Railway Diagram 603 tramcar 8.

Variants of the above are all available as part of dedicated train packs.

A three-wagon pack of private owner wagons, reflecting characters' imagined businesses from the film, is also marketed.

And not only is Titfield's railway represented, but so too road: Pearce & Crump's Bedford OB Double Vista Coach GAM 338 is also in the manufacturing pipeline.

It should be noted that models of Lion, the Wisbech coach, 'Loriot' and 'Toad' are also being marketed in non-Ealing Studios liveries by Rapido.

For those looking to model Titfield station, or indeed Monkton Combe, Peco has recently released a faithful scale version of its station building, laser cut in wood with detail parts in moulded plastic.

Broadening the net beyond pure Titfield products, there is are the forementioned Hattons '14XXs' which can still be found on the second-hand market, as well as Hornby's own version of Lion and the 'Loriot Y'. ∎

TITFIELD 'PRESERVED'

The Titfield Thunderbolt was very much a final fling for the Camerton branch, which had already closed to its last remaining goods-only traffic in 1951, a year before filming.

Track remained in place until 1958. Now, there is virtually no meaningful trace of the railway that the Liverpool & Manchester Railway ancient locomotive Lion helped propel to unlikely fame.

Thankfully, the 1838, Todd, Kitson & Laird-built 0-4-2 did survive. In fact, it did more than just survive, for it was returned to steam in 1980 for various celebrations and events, most memorably running over British Rail metals to reach Rocket 150 at Rainhill.

Last steamed in 1988, it has been permanently retired to the Museum of Liverpool.

No other locomotives, carriages or wagons used in the film are known to survive. Despite that, the North Norfolk Railway employed class survivors to make-up an evocative re-creation of the 'typical' branch line train (prior to its sabotage by Pearce & Crump) for a summer 2012, 60th anniversary of production event.

Mike Little-owned '14XX' No. 1450 was hired-in and repainted from lined BR green into matt black as 1401, and paired with the M&GN Society's sister 'Wisbech coach' No. 7 (albeit in Great Eastern Railway livery rather than Titfield – Mallingford Railway powder blue) and a hired-in 'Toad' brakevan owned by Andrew Goodman.

MAKING TRACKS:
THE GRAND CHALLENGE

The stage was set for the greatest challenge yet for Pete Waterman and the Railnuts to put together the biggest portable 'OO' gauge model railway for one weekend at the 2023 Great Electric Train Show. **MIKE WILD** goes behind the scenes to discover how it was done.

The idea was simple on paper: join all three Making Tracks layouts together for a one-off event at the 2023 Great Electric Train Show. Making it happen was a little more challenging!

It was in autumn 2022 that the idea of linking the three layouts came together and it became a reality when the measurements of the hall confirmed that 152ft would be available to join the trio of West Coast Main Line theme layouts as one.

At this point Making Tracks 3 was little more than a paper plan – and a long way from its debut in Chester Cathedral – but the team were already focused on the outcome at the end and determined to make it possible for exhibition visitors to see the spectacle come together on the weekend of October 14/15 2023 in Milton Keynes. It also meant that the brand-new model of Milton Keynes Central station would be in its home city for the Great Electric Train Show.

Even at the start of the construction of

Recreating a scene from the modern West Coast Main Line, Class 70 70015 leads a Freightliner working destined for Southampton through Tring Cutting (Making Tracks 1) on the final leg of its journey around the full 152ft x 14ft layout. Mike Wild.

Making Tracks 3, the team were thinking about the long-term aim. Timber and track was ordered for the new set of 11 8ft x 1ft storage yard boards which required over 700 pieces of Hornby track to be laid to create the extensive rear storage yard to operate the layout.

Meanwhile the consideration was made as to how Making Tracks 3 would join to the previous two layouts with its station boards being built to connect to transition boards between each section. However, the 152ft length meant that two of the layouts would reduce in length to make the final scene.

Making Tracks 1 made up 40ft, Making Tracks was reduced to 48ft while all of Making Tracks 2 was included with the final Kilsby Tunnel board being modified to become a straight transition into the Milton Keynes station scene with new details.

UPGRADES

Each Making Tracks layout had moved on significantly in both its appearance and hidden electrical systems as Pete and the Railnuts progressed their skills and expertise. The first used a ZIMO control system, but from Making Tracks 2 the tablet control functionality of the Roco Z21 DCC system had been introduced which allowed thousands of visitors to take the controls during the summer long Chester Cathedral Making Tracks events.

The latest Making Tracks 3 layout had set a new benchmark for the team in all respects with bespoke signalling systems and custom-made signals as well as a CAN bus network used to operate the points and signals as well as provide train detection.

To make the full 152ft layout work at the Great Electric Train Show meant carrying out a huge list of upgrades to the first two so that all three had the same control systems. For starters, all the signals on Making Tracks 1 and 2 were replaced using brand-new 3D printed designs created by the Railnuts team. They are equipped with bespoke circuit boards which are operated by the latest System2 control circuit boards from Megapoints while new detection modules »

2023 GREAT ELECTRIC TRAIN SHOW

were installed together with additional boosters to ensure the mammoth layout would be able to have enough power available to run an extensive fleet of sound equipped locomotives and rolling stock.

Scenery required an extensive refurbishment, particularly on Making Tracks 1, to make use of the latest techniques employed on Making Tracks 3. This included new grass covering, modification to the rock face in Tring Cutting, reducing the height of some scenic sections and introducing a new building site on top of Northchurch Tunnel.

With only 40ft of the original 64ft Making Tracks 1 on display, the team made quick work of the upgrades to its appearance paving the way for the same attention being placed on Making Tracks 2. The biggest project on the second layout was modification of the transition board which linked it with Making Tracks 3 using the final corner board. It was converted to a straight track board with a shortened version of Kilsby Tunnel including a model of the 90ft diameter ventilation shaft which stands above the tunnel. Reports suggest it was built to such a large diameter because engineers of the 1830s were uncertain as to how much ventilation would be needed to remove the steam and smoke from locomotives.

Like all the structures on Making Tracks, the ventilation shaft was a custom model, but few would know that it was only completed and installed on the Friday morning of the Great Electric Train Show weekend!

READY TO MOVE

Planning for the movement of Making Tracks was made well in advance of the show including a loading plan for the five Luton bodied vans which were booked to transport it to the Great Electric Train Show together with an extra day of set up time at the event location.

Everything was pre-arranged and stacked ready for the journey and at 9am on Thursday October 12 unloading of the convoy of vans began at the Marshall Arena in Milton Keynes. The team already had their assembly plan set out together with pre-cut measuring sticks to check the distance between the front and rear of the layout as well as for setting the height of the L-girder frames which support the baseboards.

By the middle of the day two thirds of the layout had been assembled and by the middle of the afternoon all 40 baseboards had been bolted together while catenary had been re-joined with installation of the removable sections across the baseboard to prepare for the first trains.

This though was the first time that the entire layout had been assembled which meant there were problems to fix including modifications to the wiring, adjustment of track joints – and all that was before the first trains could be placed on the track to fill the near 500ft of storage tracks.

At the end of the first day, Making Tracks was a running layout, but needed further adjustment at specific locations to ensure it would be at its best for the opening of the show. Come Friday and the team had a full day to finesse and finish the details including installing all the overhead lighting to enhance the view for visitors while stocking of the storage yard began with a series of trains.

OPERATION

Control of the trains remained in the hands of the Roco Z21 system, but with a brand-new

> *This though was the first time that that the entire layout had been assembled*
>
> MIKE WILD

At the opening of the show on Saturday October 14, crowds move to Making Tracks to be the first to see the full 152ft long layout. It filled the length of the hall at the Great Electric Train Show. **Jonathan Newton.**

Testing of Making Tracks ran into the early hours on Friday October 13 as it was the first time that all three layouts had ever been combined together. The layout lights highlight its size at night. **Mike Wild.**

The storage yard had nearly 500ft of train storage in total to keep a constant flow of different movements passing through the scenic section. **Jonathan Newton.**

Making Tracks was a popular exhibit at the 2023 Great Electric Train Show with viewers on all four sides. Jonathan Newton.

2023 GREAT ELECTRIC TRAIN SHOW

HORNBY MAGAZINE YEARBOOK 2024

An RHTT train top and tailed by a pair of Class 66s captures attention as it rolls through the bridges at Hillmorton Junction on Making Tracks 2. *Jonathan Newton.*

MAKING TRACKS: THE GRAND CHALLENGE TRACKPLAN (NOT TO SCALE)

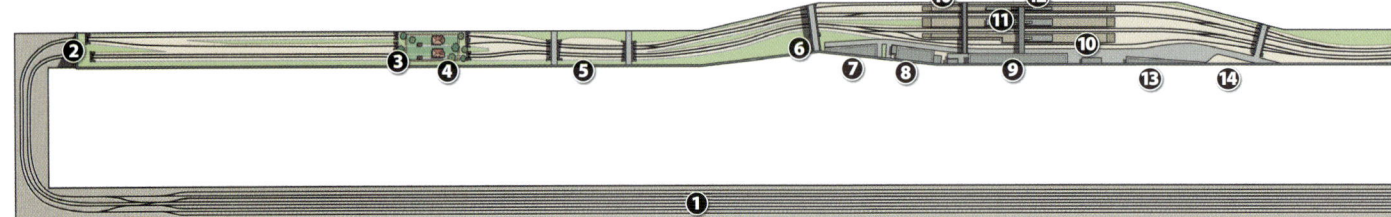

Pendolinos cross on the approach to Milton Keynes Central as a Class 70 heads south with a container train on the slow line. The length of the layout is hard to appreciate, but there is another 75ft of scenic layout ahead before the Class 70 returns to the rear storage yard. *Jonathan Newton.*

database being built across Friday to enlist the operation of the locomotives and rolling stock placed in the storage yard. Continuous testing was necessary through Friday late into the evening to iron out faults ahead of the public opening on Saturday October 14. This included multiple train operation on each circuit to ensure that enough power was available to the layout while it also confirmed how the railway would be run.

During the weekend each circuit had two drivers to keep a flow of trains running through the huge scenic area continuously. Each driver had a tablet which linked to the Z21 base station via its dedicated Wi-Fi network while each pair of tablets were dedicated to a specific circuit.

Each circuit had two tracks available in the storage yard, but to ensure operation ran smoothly only one was filled with trains for each circuit. This meant that operators could take trains from one line, run them through the scenic side and then return them to the second track in the storage yard without the need to shuffle all trains in each loop. With multiple drivers per circuit, it made for constant train movements throughout the weekend.

Rolling stock was extensive and varied, but primarily focused on the current era. On the passenger front the Class 390 Pendolinos were joined by Class 221 Super Voyagers repainted in the latest Avanti colours while just in time for the show a pair of Class 805s were completed in the recently revealed final colour scheme for the new West Coast Main Line Hitachi-built trains.

Two Caledonian Sleeper sets joined the roster with a 16-coach set running south behind a Caledonian Sleeper liveried Class 92 and a 12-coach set running north behind a GBRf liveried Class 92. There were also special trains including a super-detailed West Coast Railways 11 coach railtour set created by Richard Hall and a Riviera Trains railtour set

KEY
1. Eight-track storage yard
2. Watford Tunnel
3. Northchurch Tunnel
4. Houses
5. Tring Cutting
6. Road bridge
7. Ice rink
8. South car park
9. Station building
10. Platform
11. Canopy
12. Footbridge
13. North car park
14. Football pitch
15. Ventilation shaft
16. Kilsby Tunnel
17. Gradient to Hillmorton starts
18. Canal
19. Working catenary overlap
20. Hillmorton Junction

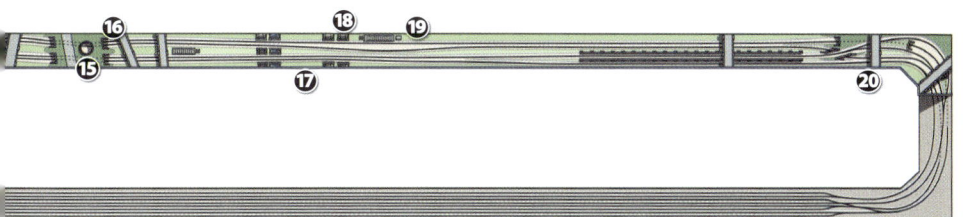

> "Making Tracks was four-deep with people of all generations"
>
> MIKE WILD

featuring a variety of Mk 1 and Mk 2 stock as seen on the real railway.

Expanding operation further for realism were light engine movements including a West Coast Railways Class 37 and preserved Gresley 'A4' 60009 *Union of South Africa* with its support coach running in between the full-length trains.

Freight stock was impressively varied and included long container trains in the hands of Class 66 and 70 diesels as well as a set hauled by a pair of Class 90s. Oil, coal, military, engineers' and cement workings were all part of the line up too with locomotives drawn from the Accurascale, Bachmann, Dapol, Heljan and Hornby collections and others.

During the weekend Making Tracks was four-deep with people of all generations watching the trains, but on Sunday evening when the show closed it was time to dismantle everything for the journey back to the Railnuts workshop.

THE FUTURE

To top off the biggest weekend in the history of Making Tracks, the layout was chosen as the winner of the Layout of the Year category in the *Hornby Magazine* Model Railway Awards which was presented to the team at the awards presentation on Saturday October 14.

However, that is far from the end of the story for Making Tracks. At Christmas, Making Tracks 3 will be operating every day from December 16-January 7 at Cheshire Outdoors at Blakemere Village near Northwich. The 64ft long model of Milton Keynes Central will be open from 10.30am-6pm each day proving another chance to see this brilliant new layout in action.

New plans are also developing for 2024 including Making Tracks attending the new Model World LIVE event at the NEC organised by Key Publishing on April 27/28. For that show the giant 152ft layout will be getting even bigger while plans are also underway for a return to the Great Electric Train Show in October 2024.

Making Tracks has had a big impact on the model railway hobby and has brought thousands of new people to see it at the Chester Cathedral and the Great Electric Train Show. The Cathedral witnessed record numbers in summer 2023 with more than 54,000 visitors flocking to see it including more than 5,000 young visitors who drove trains around the layout.

If you haven't yet seen any variants of Making Tracks shows, we can highly recommend making the pilgrimage. It's a layout of a lifetime that Pete and the Railnuts love nothing more than sharing with modellers of all ages, skill levels and interests. Keep watching *Hornby Magazine* and Key Model World for the latest news on Making Tracks and its next adventures. ∎

GBRf Class 92 92032 bursts out of Northchurch Tunnel heading north on the West Coast Main Line with the Caledonian Sleeper. Mike Wild.

2023 GREAT ELECTRIC TRAIN SHOW

STEP BY STEP: ASSEMBLING MAKING TRACKS: THE GRAND CHALLENGE

Top: With all vans on site, unloading of begins as the team prepare layout boards in the correct locations to speed assembly. **Mike Wild.**
Above: L-girder tables are assembled to a string line to set out the footprint of Making Tracks. **Jonathan Newton.**

Each baseboard has to be prepared for assembly by removing its transport boards. **Mike Wild.**

The Hillmorton Junction end (Making Tracks 2) was assembled first as the team progressed along the hall. **Jonathan Newton.**

By the middle of the day half the layout been assembled using the jigs and markers to speed the process up. **Mike Wild.**

The team assemble more of the supporting table frames for the baseboards. **Jonathan Newton.**

Northchurch Tunnel is prepared for connection to reach the full 152ft length. **Jonathan Newton.**

8 Milton Keynes Central is wider than Making Tracks 1 and 2. The boards are prepared by turning them at 90 degrees for removal of the transport packing panels. *Jonathan Newton.*

9 Catenary is reinstated across the baseboard joints to provide a continuous wire from one end to the other. *Jonathan Newton.*

10 Each piece of removable catenary is soldered in place so that the entire system can be tensioned. *Jonathan Newton.*

11 The view through Milton Keynes Central looking south during assembly of the final sections leading to Making Tracks 1. *Jonathan Newton.*

12 By Thursday evening, the first trains were running allowing testing of the track circuits and electronic systems to continue through Friday, ready for the opening of the show. *Jonathan Newton.*

58
HORNBY MAGAZINE YEARBOOK 2024

GALLERY

Masterpieces in the GALLERY

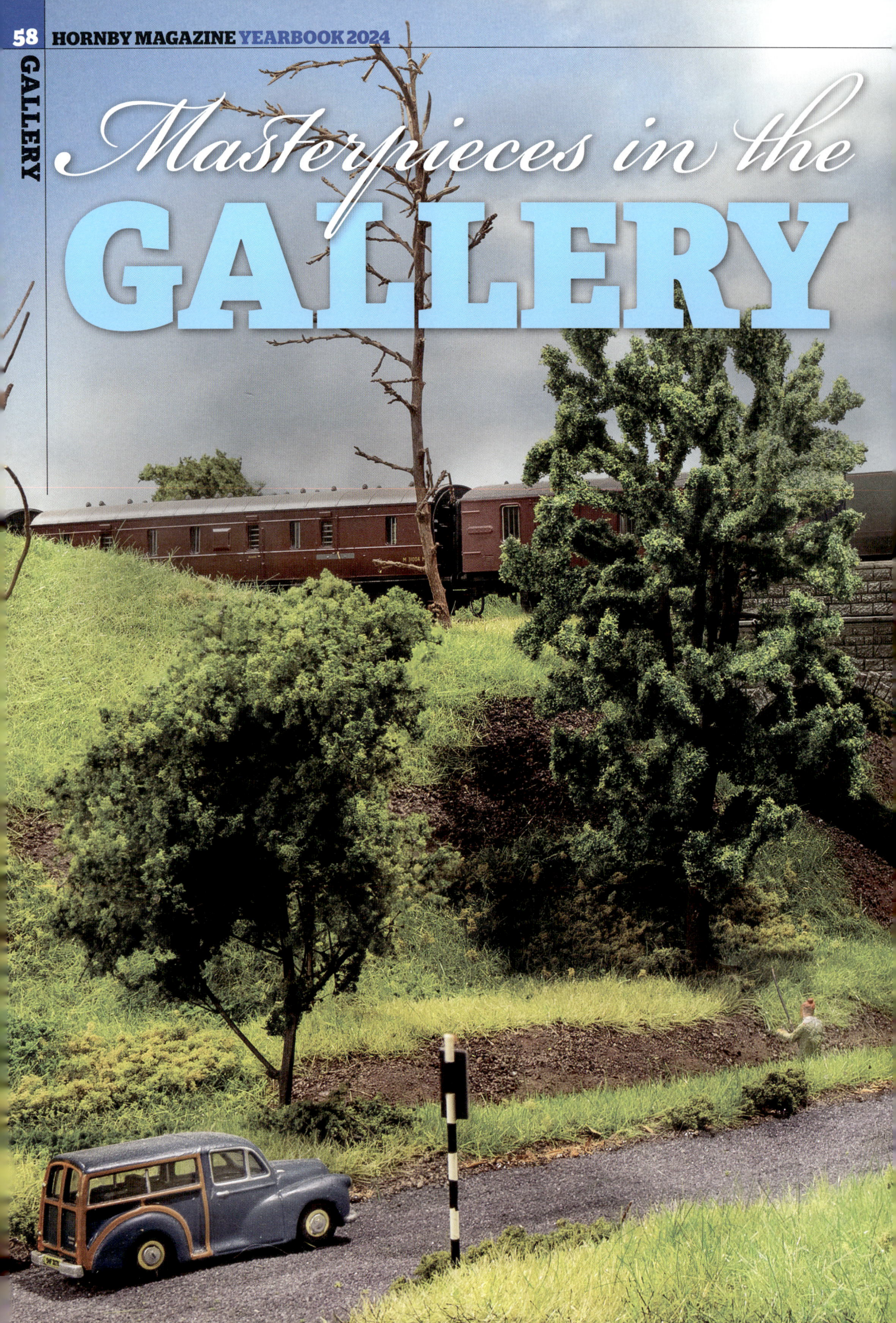

We showcase the best photography of the finest layouts from the past year. From Southern steam to 1980s diesels and back to Midland Railway steam locomotives, it has presented a stunning selection to choose from.

Bulleid 'West Country' 4-6-2 34035 Shaftsbury glides across the viaduct on the approach to Catherwood – a Southern Region terminus modelled in 'OO' gauge by Glenn Jones. Catherwood featured in HM194.
Jonathan Newton.

GALLERY

Malcolm Bentley's 'OO' gauge model of Ranelagh Bridge recreates the hydraulic era in West London with a scale model of the well-known stabling point located just outside London Paddington station. The layout featured in HM197. **Mike Wild.**

Britain's Biggest Model Railway is set to expand its scenic area in 2023-2024 as Simon George transforms the storage yard completely. Recreating a classic scene from the 1980s, 56099 in BR large logo blue powers towards Huddersfield with a loaded MGR working. Heaton Lodge Junction featured in HM196. **Mike Wild.**

GALLERY

Hawkswood Junction is Steve Brammer's home-based layout which models the BR blue diesel era with a focus on digital sound. An original BR blue and grey HST sets powers away from Hawkswood Junction. The layout featured in HM193. **Mike Wild.**

Keighley Model Railway Club's beautiful 'O' gauge layout, Coverdale, takes viewers back to the pre-grouping era. A Kirtley 0-6-0 simmers outside the goods warehouse while shunting the latest wagons for departure. Coverdale featured in HM191. **Jonathan Newton**.

Norton Saint Somers is amongst the latest scenes to be built by Stephen Fay and recreates the styling of Midsomer Norton on the Somerset and Dorset Railway. Collett '2251' 0-6-0 2211 departs with a stopping train. Norton Saint Somers featured in HM192. Jonathan Newton.

Harry Fielding selected Chinley on the Midland Main Line for his impressive 27ft x 10ft home layout. An LMS Beyer, Garratt powers a coal train while a Fowler '2P' 4-4-0 waits to depart from the bay platform. Chinley featured in HM187. Mike Wild.

Byway MPD is a compact shed scene full of character as well as the ability to represent different times of day. A Fairburn 2-6-4T and Class 03 shunter stand in the yard in the early evening at the end of the shift. Byway MPD featured in HM197. **Jonathan Newton.**

GALLERY

Misselthwaite is Lewis Bucknell's terminus station which he uses to create videos for his Mouldy Raspberry YouTube channel and links them to his second layout. A BR '4MT' 2-6-4T crosses the canal on the approach to Misselthwaite station. The layout featured in HM191. Jonathan Newton.

GALLERY

Five Elms MPD models a Southern Region steam shed between 1964 and 1967 and takes inspiration from the likes of Nine Elms. A pair of Bulleid 'Pacifics' stand boiler to boiler in the company of a BRCW Type 3 and a Bulleid 'Q1' 0-6-0. Five Elms featured in HM197. Trevor Jones.

Scarlington is the NOEL Group's current 'N' gauge exhibition layout and features a busy scene set in the 1980s and 1990s. Stanier 'Duchess' 4-6-2 46229 *Duchess of Hamilton* powers through the station at the head of a railtour. Scarlington featured in HM192. Jonathan Newton.

Martin Reynolds' Witham models a Western Region junction station with gradients at each end. A GWR 'Large Prairie' departs as a Class 117 DMU draws to a halt alongside and a '14XX' 0-4-2T draws away onto the branch line. Witham featured in HM188. **Mike Wild**.

A Bulleid rebuilt 'West Country' 4-6-2 rolls into Vale – the second station on Glenn Jones' Southern Region branch line layout. Vale featured in HM195. **Jonathan Newton**.

SUBSCRIBE TODAY!

SAVE OVER £22.00

From the Publisher
Mike Wild

Here at *Hornby Magazine* we are all at the heart of the hobby and in every issue we bring you the latest model railway news, product reviews and features you won't find anywhere else.

Each issue of the magazine is packed full of inspirational modelling articles from our dedicated team to give you all the information you need to build your own model railway or inform you about your next purchase.

Don't miss out on this great subscription offer.

Dan Evason's diorama shows how three adaptable kits can be combined to create a believable warehouse scene.

NORTH LIGHT FACTORY BACKDROP

North Light factories are a classic railway backdrop and the Key Model World Shop offers an exclusive laser-cut PJM Models kit for 'OO' gauge. **DAN EVASON** tackles two four-bay and a single-bay entrance kits to create an authentic factory façade.

Industrial backdrops are ideal for model railway scenes. They can create a reason for a siding or spur, giving a model even greater purpose and reality. However, sometimes we don't have all the space we would like to create a full factory, which is where the advantage of a low-relief model comes through.

In this modelling guide we are assembling, painting and installing three of the exclusive laser-cut North Light factory kits – available from PJM Models via the Key Model World Shop. These are supplied in a choice of two formats: a four-bay structure without doors and a single bay entrance kit as an optional add-on.

The kits have been designed to accommodate multiples being joined together and include optional parts for the ends of the roof flashing. This means that the buildings can be butted-up against one another. Alternatively, if you just want to use one building, there are end parts that allow just that.

Each kit also comes with options for the circular roof lights including a 3D printed vent, glazed window and bricked-up opening. In the four-bay kit there are also options for glazed, bricked and panelled windows to add a little variety to the finished structures.

The kits are designed to be simple and quick to assemble, but some consideration needs to be made to painting during assembly, especially as some areas do get tricky to paint once the building is complete.

Also worthy of note is that the designer has gone to town to offer full brick engraving to the inner walls as well as the outer structure for the North Light windows. This means these low relief buildings would be equally at home at the front of a layout with interior detail as they would at the rear.

The diorama for this set of buildings depicts a run-down siding outside the factory which sets the building into a typical railway scene. However, you could instead choose to have road served instead depending on the design of your own layout. ■

GRAB AN EXCLUSIVE!
Both kits are available now from www.keymodelworld.com/shop

MAKING A SCENE

TOOLS

- Deluxe Materials Rocket card glue
- Deluxe materials Ballast Bond
- Superglue
- Grey primer (All: Halfords)
- Red primer
- Grey primer
- Matt lacquer
- Fitter's cupboard (Modelu 2742)
- Fitter's Bench (Modelu 2741)
- Staff shed staff (Modelu 1006)
- Dawley Rowney (All: The Range)
- Burnt Sienna
- Burnt Umber
- Orche Yellow
- Burnt Grass (Woodland Scenics T44)
- Burnt green flock (WSScenics)
- Olive green flock (WSScenics)

STEP BY STEP: MAKE A LOW-RELIEF FACTORY BUILDING

Skill Level: Intermediate

1. It important to familiarise yourself with the pieces of the kit. There is mixture of beautifully laser cut plywood, MDF, card and acrylic. I found the instructions easy to understand, with coloured images and numbered parts map.

2. I started by creating the north light roof structures using Deluxe Materials Rocket card glue. This requires the roof frame work, windows and roofs themselves taking note of the correct orientation of the roof panels for the locating lugs.

3. I set about painting sections in order to make life easier, especially as this kit comes with interior brickwork which will be harder to access once assembled. I used red spray primer for the roof structures, white for the walls and grey for the floors.

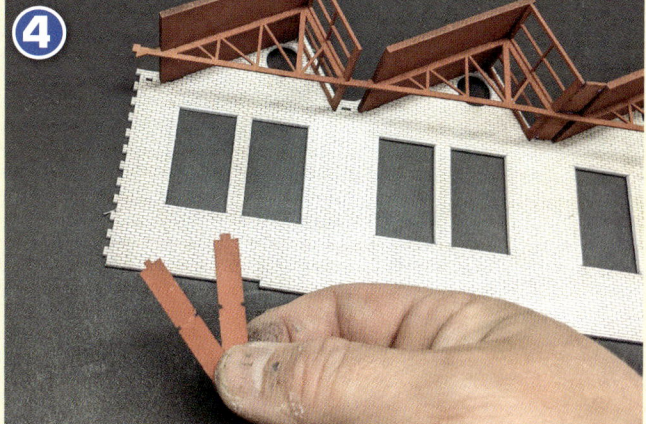

4. With the paint now dry, the main sections of the roof were glued and slotted into place using Rocket glue, before the fill-in parts plugged the horizonal planes.

STEP BY STEP: MAKE A LOW-RELIEF FACTORY BUILDING

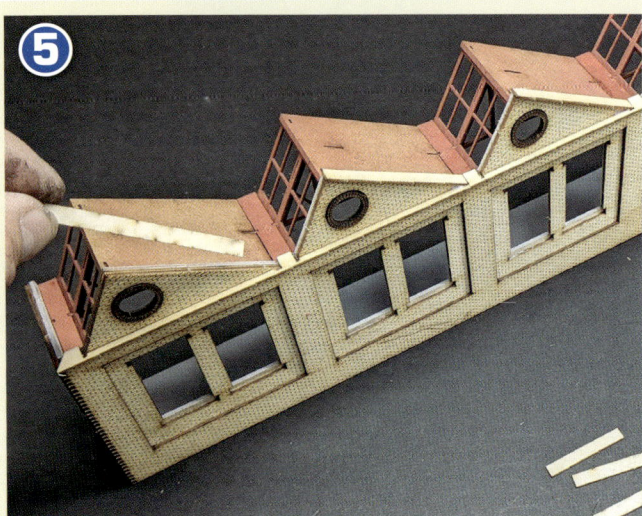

5 The sidewalls and floor were added along with the double brick front facia. A lovely little detail to this kit is the capping stones. At this point there is an option to add the capping stones on both ends depending whether you are building a standalone factory, or in my case a series of buildings joined together.

▼ I decided to add the optional warehouse doorway kit. This was constructed in same method as the main factory, starting with the roof trusses.

6

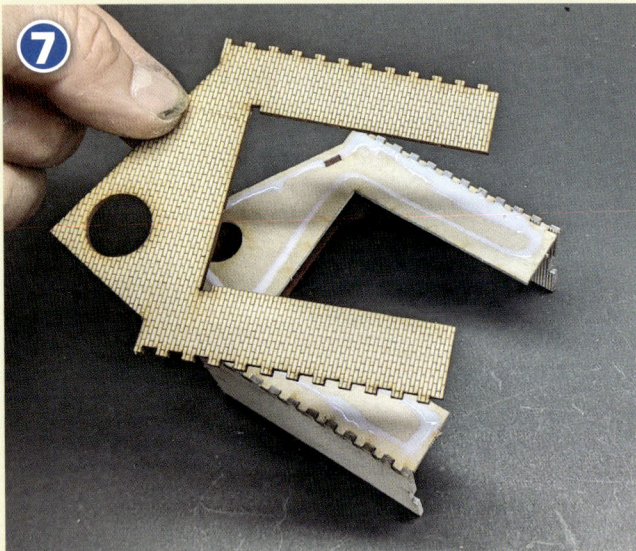

7 It is vital to pay attention to the alignment of joints and doorways; once the glue has set there is very little that can be done to fix any problems which occur.

8 The end stone cappings were fitted either side of the doorway structure and the extremities of the factory. Once complete, the trio of buildings were glued together and left to dry.

9 Next, I set about painting the brickwork using Dawley Rowney acrylic paint (Burnt Umber, Burnt Sienna, and Ochre Yellow). Using a large brush, I set about stippling the brick, mix-and-matching colours as I went along to give a random brick effect.

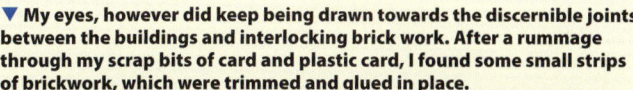

⑩ Using Vallejo light sea grey, I set about painting the capping stones. This was really when I could start to see the model come to life.

▼ My eyes, however did keep being drawn towards the discernible joints between the buildings and interlocking brick work. After a rummage through my scrap bits of card and plastic card, I found some small strips of brickwork, which were trimmed and glued in place.

⑫ Once again it was out with the paint brush and the Dawley Rowney paint and I set about matching the brickwork for a seamless finish.

▼ Next was the huge job of painting what felt like a million window sills and lintels. To make the job a lot easier, I used a strip of folded back masking tape attached to a small bit of wood sticky side up. With the sills and lintels tacked on, and armed with a large paint brush, loaded with Vallejo light sea grey, I painted them all in one go.

▼ Dawley Rowney Buff Titanium is the basis of the mortar, quickly applied with a pre-wetted brush. At this point you may think you have trashed your model, but trust, me keep going! While still wet, use a finger to wipe most of it off (a tissue removes too much), while a damp cotton bud is useful for the hard-to-reach areas.

⑭ After drying, the sills and lintels were pressed the into place. They are such a good fit that I didn't need glue, but you can add a drop for extra security. I then sealed the brickwork with Halfords matt lacquer.

STEP BY STEP: MAKE A LOW-RELIEF FACTORY BUILDING

16 With the paint now dry, I set about fitting windows frames and glazing. The inner window frames were fitted first, followed by the pre-cut glazing panels. I then fitted the window frames on top. The frames were painted a light cream colour to finish.

17 Different options are included for the upper portholes: vents open, glazed windows or grilled vents. For the main factory I went with windows (carefully pressed in from the rear), on the open door I went with a grilled vent option (fitted from the front of the building).

▼ With the tiles now trimmed down using a sharp scalpel, I painted the gutter areas using a dark grey to mimic real life lead in real life.

18 The roof tiles come in a pre-cut strips, with the added bonus of being printed on dark grey/black card. However, a splash of grey and white primer improves the texture. When the tiles were dry, I set about cutting them from their fret and applied strips using card glue.

19

▼ Once the gutters and down pipes were dry, they were carefully superglued into place.

20 Although not included in the kit, I decided to add my own down pipes and gutter points between the pitches of the roofs. These were simply made using styrene square strips cut into small rectangle blocks and using some small gauge wire for the down pipes which was snipped to length. These were then sprayed into with red primer.

21

There's no skimping on the interior, which is offered in full relief and ripe for individual detailing.

With the building now complete it was time to create a little diorama around it on a scrap of leftover wood. I trimmed a length of Peco bullhead track and glued it in place.

I added a homemade mix of ballast and grey tile grout. This was dampened down with Deluxe Ballast Bond applied and left overnight to dry.

With the ballast now dry I added a dusty track alongside the railway and the factory. Using course sandpaper, I gently sanded down the road giving the ballast a lighter effect as if tyres been driven over it. I used the airbrush and applied Tamiya hull red to the rails.

▼ With the greenery now dry and the excess removed, I used WWS light earth weathering powder and gently blended the gravel road into the grassy areas with a medium size paintbrush.

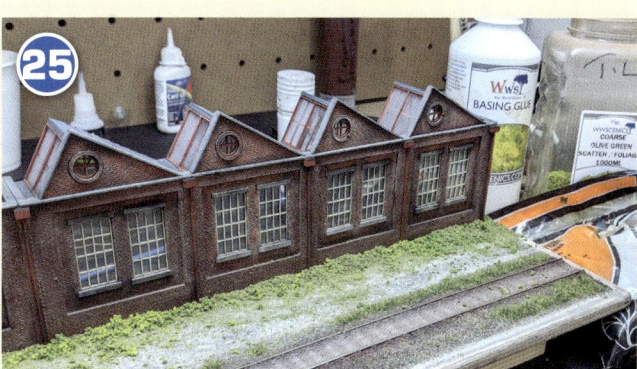

Rough ground was added the scene with a mixture of static grass, flocks and scatters on dabs of PVA. The more random the effect the better. I also glued the building into place using the flocks and scatter to bed it in, and to make it look like it has been there for many years.

With Modelu offering a fantastic range of industrial figures, workbenches and cupboards, I set about painting and placing them in place. I also used some of Scale Model Scenery's downloadable 'OO' posters, again to add personal touches.

The original: *Cock o' the North* is posed for its official Doncaster Works portrait in 1934. **A1 Trust**

BUILDING A LEGEND: THE GRESLEY 'P2' 2-8-2

Modern design methods and a brand-new facility are helping to shape construction of Britain's most powerful steam locomotive in Darlington. **MIKE WILD** meets A1 Steam Trust Chairman **STEVE DAVIES MBE** to find out how the mammoth project to scratch-build an LNER 'P2' 2-8-2 is progressing.

DARLINGTON is the birth place of so many railway locomotives. It was at the centre of railway engineering until the 1960s, but even though the history of the town has vanished in many cases, the A1 Steam Locomotive Trust is rekindling such construction with the opening of its brand-new workshop and a clear vision for the future.

The A1 Trust is already well established and known for its impressive and high-profile building of Peppercorn 'A1' 4-6-2 60163 *Tornado* – a missing link in East Coast Main Line preservation. Since its completion in 2008, it has been seen across the country, featured in a race from King's Cross to Edinburgh Waverley alongside a period bike and car on BBC's *Top Gear*, hauled main line timetabled ('Plandampf') passenger trains over the Settle – Carlisle route and, amazingly, became the first steam locomotive to nudge 100mph since the end of steam in the 1960s.

However, all that is just the start for the A1 Trust. It is progressing with construction of a brand-new 'P2' 2-8-2 2007 *Prince of Wales*. Indeed, its sights are already set on a new-build Gresley 'V4' 2-6-2 3403 *Highlander* once the 'Mikado' is completed.

The new works facility is a world away from the previous site on North Road, even though it is within striking distance. That was the old Stockton and Darlington Railway carriage works, but the new location – just across the Tees Valley Line at North Road station – is state of the art and includes space inside for maintenance and construction, a viewing gallery and a vision for the future of main line steam in the North East.

"Here we will build, we will repair and we will be able to service main line steam as we have a main line connection going in, plus we will have a turntable," says A1 Trust Chairman Steve Davies MBE.

The famous 'A1' *Tornado* is currently undergoing a thorough overhaul to prepare it for another stint on the national network, and, on the day of our visit to the new Darlington Locomotive Works, the boiler was raising steam for testing in the yard. The frames and tender are at Locomotive Maintenance Services, Loughborough (close to the Great Central Railway), and it will soon be reassembled paving the way for the team to refocus on the Gresley 'P2' build.

Although incomplete, the carcass of the new 'P2' is already imposing.
All pictures: Mike Wild (unless stated)

NEW BUILD 'P2'

> *"The 'P2' is like Mount Everest – we are doing it because it there to be done."*
> **STEVE DAVIES MBE**

BRITAIN'S MOST POWERFUL STEAM LOCOMOTIVE

The Gresley 'P2' is a huge project, not least because the Trust is working to resolve the issues of the original Gresley design including modification of the leading pony truck, changes to the cylinder block design to fit the modern railway and changes to the valve gear to make the locomotive more efficient.

"Main line drivers are queuing up to drive the 'P2,'" comments Trust Chairman Steve Davies – and that's even before the locomotive is completed. "There is nothing else like the 'P2' and once it is running it will be without doubt the most powerful steam locomotive in Britain," he adds. "We expect it to generate over 3,000hp."

That target is huge. It represents almost the same power output as a Class 60 or 66 heavy freight diesel from a steam locomotive, and one which will have huge presence with its eight-driving wheels and distinctive Gresley 'W1' style front end.

The real 'P2' locomotives were introduced in 1934 for the torturous Edinburgh – Aberdeen route in Scotland. This demanding route with its gradients and curves demanded a more powerful locomotive and Gresley chose the 2-8-2 wheel arrangement to deliver maximum power to the rails within the limits of the turntable length. Only six were built – 2001-2006 – with the first featuring Lentz rotary cam valve gear.

Magnificent though these locomotives were, they weren't without their troubles. Drifting steam caused visibility issues for the crews, while the pony truck design was the cause of derailments at slow speed and there were draughting problems with the cylinder block which caused heat transfer between the cylinders and the exhaust, losing efficiency. In selecting to build a brand-new 'P2', the A1 Steam Trust set out to resolve the inherent problems.

None of the original locomotives survived. All were rebuilt in the late 1940s by Thompson as the 'A2/2' 4-6-2s, and all were scrapped. This history of lament helps the 'P2' fit in with the A1 Steam Trust outlook: "We only build engines which don't exist," confirms Steve. "The 'P2' is like Mount Everest – we are doing it because it there to be done."

MODERN STEAM LOCOMOTIVE DESIGN

Building a steam locomotive today is very different to the world in which Darlington Works once operated. Almost everything is a one-off part, but there are advantages to the modern era which can help as well, not least modern design technology.

The new Darlington Locomotive Works has doubled the trust's workspace.

Eight coupled wheels... now for the valve gear!

Much of the pipework has already been fitted; a learning from the construction of 'A1' 60163 *Tornado* when some was left until after the boiler was fitted.

The fabricated cylinder block, based on the original monobloc, is a staggering piece of 21st century engineering. **A1 Trust**

The big items keep on coming... this is the almost-finished boiler inside Germany's Meiningen Works. **A1 Trust**

"The integration of steam with the modern digital railway has been an interesting exercise"
STEVE DAVIES MBE

The 'A1' was designed with two-dimensional Computer Aided Design (CAD) drawings, but the 'P2' has the added advantage of three-dimensional design. "The 'P2' has been designed with 3D CAD which has given us the confidence that every part we design and build off site will fit," confirms Steve.

Right now, the 'P2' is mid-way through construction. The frames, smokebox, cab and basic running gear are all complete, making it a rolling locomotive. That leaves three particularly significant missing components: the boiler, cylinder block and valve gear. The fabricated 'monobloc' is now complete and been through through pressure testing with specialist manufacturer Howco, but the boiler and valve gear, design changes have been necessary.

Like the 'A1', the new boiler for the 'P2' is being built in Germany by Meiningen Works, but cleverly the Trust has been thinking about how to make its two locomotives more efficient once they are complete by using the same design as that fitted to the 'A1'. "We have taken some liberties with the 'P2' as the 'A1' boiler is actually 14in shorter. The differences are hidden by the cladding," says Steve.

There is a distinct advantage to this plan as an interchangeable boiler makes overhauls simpler to achieve with the ultimate aim to have three boilers which can be switched between the two locomotives to reduce their time out of service.

The Trust is also working through amendments to the 'P2' design, lead by David Elliott. This includes modification of front pony truck which was a problem to the original locomotives at low speed: "We took the 'V2' pony truck design – an efficient design – and put that under the 'P2'," Steve adds.

Next David was tasked with revisions to the cylinder block which included changes to the design to allow it to fit the modern railway loading gauge as well as modifications to prevent heat transfer between the cylinders and exhaust. This was particularly important for the locomotive's efficiency.

"The cylinder block has been built by Howco through their experience in pressure vessels," says Steve. "The design was subjected to CAD simulations for the flow of steam and the computer showed that David had cracked the problem. The simulation also looked at the flow of steam from the chimney under different conditions, as the original engine had a problem with steam drifting."

The final major revision is to the valve gear. The 'P2' uses Lentz rotary cam gear, but as Steve explains it too suffered shortcomings: "The problem was it didn't have variable cut off, it had 10% jumps. It is like going from gear one to three in your car and has now been redesigned for gradual cut off which will improve the efficiency of the locomotive."

DIGITAL RAILWAY UPGRADES

Redesigning the steam functionality of the Gresley 'Mikado' is only one part of the story, as the 'P2' has to confirm with an increasingly technical and digital main line railway system. "The integration of steam with the modern digital railway has been an interesting exercise," comments Steve. "We are currently fitting European Train Control System (ETCS)

Shades of Doncaster? These are the tender wheelsets.

NEW BUILD 'P2'

A 'P2' in 'OO'… but with a difference. New 'Mikado' 2007 *Prince of Wales* may not yet be finished, but you can already enjoy one in miniature form, thanks to Hornby.

Here's one we made earlier! Proof, were it needed, that building a large Gresley locomotive isn't fanciful is the very existence of new Peppercorn 'Pacific' 60163 *Tornado*. Paired with the Severn Valley Railway's LNER teak train, the 'A1' accelerates away from Bridgnorth during an autumn 2015 visit.
Jack Boskett/A1 Trust

> "This engine is oven-ready; we can spend money as fast as it comes in"

STEVE DAVIES MBE

to *Tornado* and we are very proud that Network Rail entrusted us to be the first steam locomotive with ETCS."

Fitting this new technology means that the 'A1' and 'P2' (which will be fitted with the same equipment) can continue to operate into big main line terminus stations like London King's Cross which is currently in the process of being upgraded to digital, in-cab only signalling by Network Rail.

"The steam locomotive cab is incredibly hostile and with the addition of ETCS we have doubled the amount of wiring on each locomotive," Steve says. The electronics on the footplate include Train Protection and Warning System (TPWS), lighting and even the option to charge your phone from the footplate of the 'A1' or 'P2'. All of this has to be powered and the 'P2' will have a steam turbine generator in place of the original feed water heaters on the running boards to power its electrical equipment.

"One of the advantages of building a new steam locomotive is that we can design these features in from the start, rather than being stuck with remaining spaces in the frames," Steve comments.

STOCKTON AND DARLINGTON 200 DEADLINE

If building a brand-new 'P2' wasn't a big enough challenge, the A1 Trust has now set a target of having the locomotive in steam by September 2025 in order to take part in the Stockton and Darlington 200th anniversary. Steve says: "The timescale for the project is now quite tight. I want it to play a part in the Stockton and Darlington 2025 events as we are absolutely central to that with our new facility."

How can the trust achieve that? Over to Steve: "*Tornado* took about 18 years to build, but even throwing money at it, it probably wouldn't have got done any quicker. The 'P2' is different because we understand what we are doing."

We'll leave the last words to the chairman. "We can have all the plans in the world, but without money they are meaningless. We are extremely fortunate that this business model, this kind of dream factory, that the engines we are thinking about become reality and attract a lot of people who put money in regularly.

Steve adds: "Success breeds success, and it is noticeable that as a new component arrives and we advertise that, money comes in. This engine is oven-ready; we can spend money as fast as it comes in. The only thing holding us back is not technical, it's purely financial. Get your money in and you will see this locomotive banging away up Shap and Beattock sooner than you think." ■

• Discover more at www.p2steam.com

YOUR ONLINE MODELLING

Unmissable modelling inspiration at your finger tips

"A modeller's paradise"
Christopher

"The key that unlocks the world of modelling!"
Graham

- ✓ Get all the **latest news** first
- ✓ **Exclusive** product and layout videos
- ✓ Fresh **inspiration**, tips and tricks every day
- ✓ More than **5,000 searchable** modelling articles
- ✓ Back issues of **Hornby Magazine**
- ✓ Full access to **Hornby Magazine** content
- ✓ All available on **any device** - *anywhere, anytime*

Visit:
www.keymod

SCALE DESTINATION

Featuring

Exclusive video series!

NEW SERIES: Building a 'TT:120' model railway
A brand-new series is out now on Key Model World as the team embarks on its next project: a 'TT:120' scale layout. Join for this brand-new four-part series as we create Twelvemill Bridge. Don't miss it!

SERIES 5: 1960s Weathering
In our fifth series Mike Wild and Jonathan Newton show detailed techniques for weathering locomotives, carriages and wagons using powders, acrylics, washes and airbrushes. Watch the full series today.

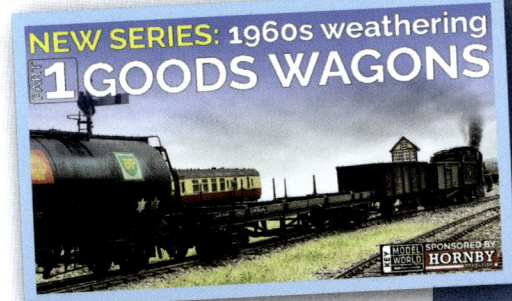

SERIES 4: Flying Scotsman Centenary
2023 marks the 100th anniversary of the world's most famous steam locomotive – 60103 Flying Scotsman. We follow the locomotive during its visit to the Keighley and Worth Valley Railway in May 2023 to discover how the legend is kept alive.

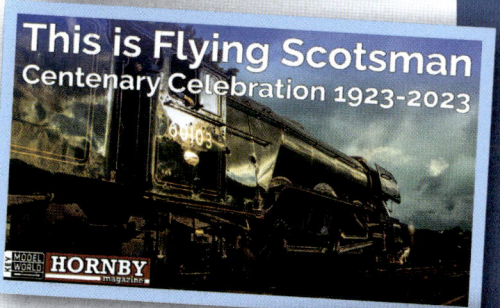

SERIES 3: Building a Diesel Depot
In our third video series we build a diesel depot using brand-new laser-cut kits from the Key Model World Shop collection in just 11ft x 2ft. Join the team as they show how you can do the same step by step.

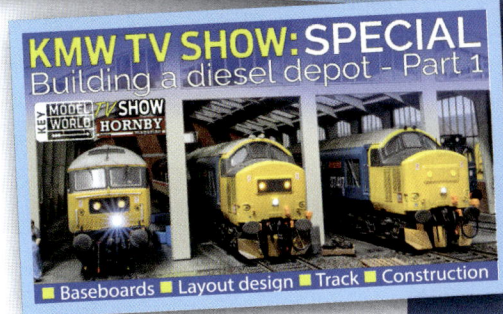

RAILWAY REALISM

ROUTE 66

One of the most recognisable locomotives currently at work in the UK is the Electro-Motive built Class 66, a type that originated in the USA and which has come to dominate our freight scene. **EVAN GREEN-HUGHES** celebrates 25 years of success.

Visit almost any main railway station in Britain and sooner or later you will come across a freight train hauled by one of the over 500 Class 66s currently at work on the network. The type is favoured by most of the major freight companies, used on everything from bulk mineral trains to container distribution services and can be seen everywhere from the south coast right to the tip of northern Scotland.

It is hard to believe that these workhorses have been with us now for a quarter of a century and also, with no universal replacement on the horizon, that they are likely to be in service for many more years to come. So successful are these locomotives that, even now, further second-hand examples are being brought into the country and, in some cases, they are actually taking over work previously done by electric locomotives, due to the high cost of mains power.

The Class 66 story began in the early 1980s when Somerset quarry operator Foster Yeoman placed an order with Electro-Motive (EMD) for a small fleet of freight locomotives which were intended to haul heavy aggregate trains over long distances. The order went to the USA because of its extensive experience in building heavy freight locomotives and could promise levels of reliability and haulage capacity that British manufacturers could not match. In the event, these locomotives, the

Freightliner has made full use of the General Motors Type 5 with its first locomotives entering service in 2000. On April 20 2023 66588 leads 4O90 Leeds FCT-Southampton down the East Coast Main Line a few miles north of Peterborough on April 20 2023. **MIKE WILD.**

Class 59s, were a revelation, performing even better than the builders had promised, and setting reliability levels that had never been achieved by existing motive power.

When the railways were privatised around ten years later, there was to be more American influence still. This time, a consortium led by Wisconsin Central Transportation Systems acquired virtually the whole of the UK freight network, promising to modernise and streamline the operation with a view to bringing it back to profitability. It was named English, Welsh and Scottish Railways (EWS).

EWS acquired around 1,600 locomotives with the freight operation, although not all were in working order, and of these the bulk were more than 30 years old and dated from British Railways' original modernisation plan. Reliability of the fleet was appalling: most were available for work only about 65% of the time, and technicians who visited from the USA were said to be taken aback at the amount of oil and contamination to be found in UK-built locomotives' engine rooms.

Last built Class 66, GBRf operated 66779, leads a very lightly loaded 4M23 from Felixstowe North-Hams Hall on the approach to King Street Crossing, Helpston, on January 21 2023. This locomotive marked the end of Class 66 production and received BR green livery as well as being named *Evening Star* at the National Railway Museum. **Mike Wild.**

UNDER THE BONNET

Clearly something had to be done, especially as the new company wanted to reduce its overheads with a view to becoming more competitive, recognising that one of the ways this could be done was to improve the efficiency of its locomotive fleet.

It was decided that the only way that proper efficiency could be achieved would be to virtually replace all of the company's stock, but for this plan to work each new engine would have to replace around five of the old ones, which in itself indicated that a very high level of availability would be required. EWS therefore looked at the experience gained by the Somerset quarry operation and approached EMD with a list of its requirements. These included a top speed of 75mph along with a wide route gauge/weight range and availability of more than 90%.

EMD came back with a design that was an amalgamation of several types. The body was derived from the Class 59, and indeed looked very similar to the earlier engines, in order to reduce the number of issues in getting the class certified to run on the UK network.

The intended power unit was a 12-cylinder two stroke diesel which was of a design that the company had been producing for more than 20 years, rather than the 16-cylinder version that had been used on the Class 59. Meanwhile, the control equipment was similar to that which had been used on Irish Rail's 201 Class locomotives.

Underneath the heavy solebar a new type of bogie would be fitted, which incorporated radial steering, designed to reduce wheel and rail wear while EMD's revolutionary creep control, which controlled wheelslip would be included. Cab design was very similar to the Class 59, and the fuel capacity was set at 1,800 gallons, enabling long periods of service between refuelling.

EWS was evidently happy with the proposal and in May 1996 placed an order for 250 locomotives at a total cost of £375m, straight off the drawing board. Design work was completed only five months after that and construction of the first example got under way in May the following year at the General Motors plant in Ontario, Canada.

In the first full year of Class 66 operation, 66094 tows Class 37s 37713 and 37513 through Stratford on August 23 1999 at the head of a westbound freight. **Mike Wild.**

DB Cargo has taken over operation of the former EWS Class 66s and an increasing amount are appearing in its corporate red and grey colour scheme. Class 66 66134 passes through Whitley Bridge with biomass hoppers destined for Drax on April 21 2021. **Mike Wild.**

NEW JERSEY TO LINCOLNSHIRE

The first locomotive, 66001, was ready in a commendably short space of time, first taking to the rails in early 1997, before being taken to New Jersey where it was put on a ship for its voyage to the UK.

After arrival at Immingham docks, the class doyen was unloaded with the press invited to view it before it was taken to Toton depot for commissioning, crew familiarisation and trials.

The locomotive worked its first revenue-earning train within six weeks of its arrival, with all tests being considered successful.

A second locomotive, 66002, was also completed and this was taken to a test centre in Colorado, USA, where it acquitted itself with flying colours, arriving in the UK some months later. The performance of the first two locomotives was exactly as the manufacturer had promised and this then enabled the company to embark on construction of the remainder of the order.

Progress on this was very swift indeed and 11 locomotives would arrive on each ship at a time. All of these had been pre-tested so that all engineers in the UK had to do was to connect the batteries, unpin the suspension and top-up the fuel tanks before putting the 66s to work. The whole order was completed and delivered by June 2000 after just 26 months, enabling a large number of older and less economical locomotives to be taken out of service in quick order.

The success of EWS's Class 66s was noted with keen interest by other UK freight operators, which were beginning to expand. One was Freightliner, a company that already had some of its Class 47s fitted with General Motors power units. It decided to take an initial order for five Class 66s in March 1999, and upped this to a total of 20 shortly afterwards, delivered alongside the final examples for EWS. Numbered in the 66/5 series, these were identical to the EWS version and immediately showed their worth on long-distance container trains as well as aggregate traffic, allowing older locomotives, such as the Class 47 to be withdrawn.

The next customer for the Class 66 was GB Railways, which decided to move into the freight market in 2000 as GB Railfreight (GBRf). To enable this transition, it placed an order for seven examples. Numbered in the 66/7 series, these were again identical to both the EWS and the Freightliner versions and were intended initially for use on network infrastructure work, but later spread their wings to other duties. These engines landed

66716 Willesden Traincare Centre approaches Wansford, Nene Valley Railway, with a London Underground driver training special on September 12 2006. GBRf was using the NVR to train Underground drivers on Class 66s following the start of a contract for GBRf to supply 66 power for engineering trains. **Mike Wild.**

RAILWAY REALISM

Main: The Class 66 was designed for use on a wide range of freight traffic types and work across the British railway system. On February 9 2006, EWS Class 66 66198 approaches Whittlesey, Cambridgeshire, with a loaded aggregates train. *Mike Wild.*
Above: Direct Rail Services is another user of the Class 66 with a fleet of Class 66/4 locomotives on its books. On June 13 2023 66430 speeds north through Milton Keynes Central with a lengthy northbound container train. *Mike Wild.*

at Newport docks in March 2001 and, as we customary, were immediately put to work.

Following these batches came another series for Freightliner, but this time there were some mechanical changes which saw a lower gear ratio used, with the effect of reducing the maximum speed but increasing the haulage capacity, making them more suitable for aggregate traffic. As a result of the changes, these 25 locomotives were numbered in the 66/6 series.

In 2002 a further operator began to order Class 66s. Direct Rail Services had until this point used a number of different classes of first-generation diesels on its mainly nuclear fuel traffic, but needed to update its ageing fleet. The Carlisle based firm eventually had 14 constructed, but later added to their fleet by taking some from EWS (by this time rebranded as DB Cargo).

EUROPE AND BEYOND
At this point it is worth adding to the story that similar locomotives to the Class 66 were also constructed for use in Europe and Africa from 1998 onwards. These have seen service in France, Poland, the Benelux countries, Germany, Sweden, Denmark and Egypt. Around 200 non-UK examples have been built. Although these are not all of the same variant, all have the same appearance as the UK machines, apart from the fitting of additional air conditioning units above the cabs on some examples.

It was at this point that it became necessary to change the specification of the Class 66. This was owing to a ruling from the International Union of Railways on emissions levels, and this led to a lower-emission version being brought into service, with an update of the engine, the 12N-710G3B-U2, being substituted for the original. This version had many changes, particularly to the cooling system, which took up more internal space and meant that an extra external door had to be added to the bodywork, because it was no longer possible to enter the engine room from the cab at one end. This uprated locomotive first made an appearance with Freightliner's 66952 in April 2004, followed by 66951.

Class 66s built to this design can be identified by their slightly smaller fuel tanks.

As indicated by the large number of orders placed, the Class 66 proved to be a highly-successful locomotive, although not without its problems.

The biggest of these was driver comfort, or lack of, with complaints made about cab noise, vibration and heat levels, while there was also criticism of the control layout which were set out in American style with the power controller and associated equipment on a pedestal at the side of the driver, rather than being incorporated into a desk, as was usual here.

Several changes have been made since with some of these being specific to individual operators, particularly GBRf which used a new cab layout with a proper desk in locomotives from 66708 onwards.

Issues with the bogies in the early days were more quickly sorted, and proved to be the only significant mechanical problem suffered.

Orders for the 66 kept on coming. A new operator, Fastline Freight bought six, although that was

GB Railfreight has brought a broad spectrum of unique colour schemes to the Class 66 including BR Railfreight and BR large logo. GBRf 66789 *British Rail 1948-1997* rounds the curve from the Werrington Dive Under to Glinton Junction with 6E88 - Middleton Towers-Goole Glass Works - on April 24 2023. Mike Wild.

short-lived as the company soon went bust, with these half-dozen split acquired by DRS.

GBRf ordered another 21 in 2013, but were built at a different plant, this time Muncie, Indiana, USA. Further reductions in emissions were bring imposed and this led to a further order for seven locomotives, with these using six spare power units, along with one recovered from 66734, which had been scrapped after an accident. The reason was that existing power units were exempt the new regulations, as long as they were already in the EU, but it did mean that they had to be transported to America for fitting.

As it turned out, the batch that used the reallocated power units (66752-779) were to be the last Class 66s built new for this country. The locomotive's design could not easily be changed to accommodate the additional equipment that had been specified for the next stage of emission reduction and so production ended in 2014.

MIX AND MATCH

With so many Class 66s built, it is not surprising that some have been swapped between operators as demand has changed. Colas Rail took five locomotives from Freightliner and renumbered them in the 66/8 series while Freightliner has taken seven that used to be with DRS and retain their original numbers. DRS has five that started life with EWS, while GBRF has a total of 14 that were originally in service with other operators.

With production of new class 66s now banned, attention has turned to overseas to satisfy home demand for one company. GBRF has been importing locomotives from Europe and has been having them converted to full UK specification before repainting and renumbering them in the 66/3 series. These have all come from leasing company Akiem, which originally started off with seven class 66s used by Veolia Cargo and Crossrail Benelux. The company later obtained further 66s when it took over Macquarie European Rail, but made them available when the original leases on them ran out.

GBRf operates around 100 Class 66s built in several batches including some sourced from overseas operators. 66730 heads 4M47 London Gateway GBRf-Hams Halll GBRf on June 13 2023 at Milton Keynes. Mike Wild.

The Class 66s capabilities are extensive and allow them to be used on long distance container trains as well as heavy and intensive short distance flows such as iron ore from Immingham Docks to Scunthorpe. On July 12 2018 66524 heads the 15.04 Immingham Dock ore terminal-Scunthorpe ore plant at Barnetby. **Mike Wild.**

Conversely, Freightliner has transferred several of its Class 66s in the other direction to its Polish subsidiary Freightliner PL and modified to European specification. EWS also moved around 60 locomotives to France for service with its subsidiary EuroCargoRail a decade ago, although these are sometimes seen back in this country for maintenance. A further 15 locomotives were sent to Poland for use by another subsidiary, DB Schenker Rail Polska, including one of the machines that had already been at work in France.

As can be seen the demand for the Class 66 continues to be high and, despite their advancing age, the locomotives are still putting in impressive levels of reliability, which still surpass all other freight locomotives in use both in this country and abroad. Several have now joined the ranks of railway celebrities, particularly last-built 66779, which was outshopped in British Railways green livery and named *Evening Star* as a homage to the last steam engine produced for our railways some 53 years earlier. Another particular favourite at the moment is 66789 which appeared in large logo BR blue in February 2018, and also 66793 which wears the attractive sectorisation two-tone grey livery. Others appear in a multitude of liveries, including Colas, GBRF, DRS, EWS, DB Rail and several versions of Freightliner, making them all the more attractive to modellers of the modern era.

Today almost all the Class 66s built survive in service, the only exceptions to this being 66521 which was written off in the Great Heck accident of February 2001; 66048 which crashed at Carrbridge in January 2010; and 66734 which derailed at Loch Treig in June 2012 and had to be cut up on site. Others are temporarily out of use depending on requirements.

The Class 66 was brought into this country by an American company determined to show that diesel locomotives could be more efficient and economical than had ever been previously thought possible. This they succeeded in doing to the extent that no freight locomotives have been built in this country ever since, and probably now never will be. The fact that there is no replacement on the horizon suggests that the Class 66 still has a long future ahead of it, here and abroad. ■

PROTOTYPE DIESELS

BREAKING THE MOULD!

They were the rarest of diesels and until relatively recently unheard of in ready-to-run model form. **NICK BRODRICK** charts the remarkable prototype locomotives, full size and miniature.

Once upon a time, you'd never have dared dream that one of the mainstream manufacturers would issue models of any prototype diesels. Rare, niche and unusual, these one-offs, or certainly no more than trio runs, would have been too great a risk to invest the considerable sums required to make a 'OO' version.

That all changed in 2008 when new models of *Deltic* and *Falcon* were released – and sold well. It has taken 15 years, but now all 13 rarities are now available off the shelf, with Heljan's LMS 10800 released in 2023.

Perhaps it's no surprise that prototype diesels have great appeal. Not only do they add considerable interest to any layout (in sometimes striking colours), but they are also firmly embedded in the final two decades' of the steam era, meaning that a lot of changeover years modellers can justify at least one!

Diesel prototypes offer unique locomotives with one of the most striking being Heljan's model of BRCW Type 4 D0260 *Lion* in white. Mike Wild.

PROTOTYPE DIESELS

LMS 10000 AND 10001 (BUILT 1947-1948)
In 'OO' form: Bachmann/Rails of Sheffield (2015) and Dapol (2011)
With Nationalisation on the horizon, the London, Midland & Scottish Railway was still keen to be at the forefront of locomotive design and technology.

Derby Works was just in the nick of time to roll out the company's debut express diesel locomotive, 10000, in November 1947, ensuring that the LMS legend was emblazoned on the bodysides in full stainless steel 'bling'.

Unveiling of 10000 the following month coincided with the naming of 'Princess Coronation' 6256 *Sir William A Stanier FRS* at Euston, in the presence of the former LMS Chief Mechanical Engineer himself. Runs between St Pancras, Derby and Manchester followed.

It was the first of two prototypes; 10001 emerged in July 1948, now under British Railways ownership, and though it carried the same black and silver livery, it did not have LMS lettering and its predecessor's 'Big Four' branding was removed, somewhat belatedly, in November 1951.

Both 1,600 horse power locomotives (fitted with English Electric engines) were used double-headed between Euston and Carlisle Citadel in summer 1948, but in subsequent years were used singularly both on St Pancras and Euston trains.

The Southern Region adopted the 'LMS twins' in 1953-1955 and were used interchangeably on Waterloo – Bournemouth and Exeter services, before being returned to their native London Midland Region.

Repainting into BR green followed which is the form that 10000-10001 remained in service until their respective withdrawals in 1966 and 1963. Sadly, neither survived the cutter's torch, but the Wirksworth-based Ivatt Diesel Recreation Society is steadily making a replica using parts salvaged from other locomotive classes.

PROTOTYPE DIESELS

BR(W) 18000 (BUILT 1949)
In 'OO' form: Heljan (2021)

Nicknamed 'Kerosene Castle', Gas Turbine locomotive No. 18000 was originally ordered by the Great Western Railway from the Brown Boveri in Switzerland in 1940. But it would be 1949 before the A1A-A1A would arrive on British shores.

After commissioning at Swindon Works, the 'double-red route' restricted (115 ton) No. 18000 began to haul expresses between Paddington and Plymouth. This necessitated tests over the arduous South Devon Banks, which were not entirely successful – at least as much as BR's Western Region would have liked – and hopes that the gas turbine would be able to shift 350 tons unaided had to be scaled back to just shy of 300 tons.

Nevertheless, No. 18000 continued to give reliable service until withdrawal in December 1960 by when it had been declared uneconomic to operate and stored at Swindon.

It survived scrapping thanks to its re-use by the European Office for Research and Development back in Switzerland, minus its gas turbine and was shipped back to the continent in January 1964. The unpowered test bed was eventually put on display at the Mechanical Engineering Testing building in Vienna, Austria.

That was before the one-off locomotive was brought back to the UK for preservation in the 1990s under the ownership of Pete Waterman and initially kept at Crewe Heritage Centre. It was placed on loan to Didcot in 2011 and cosmetic restoration to original British Transport Commission black and chrome trim is about to get underway having been latterly exhibited in BR green.

PROTOTYPE DIESELS

BR(M) 10800 (BUILT 1950)
In 'OO' form: Heljan (2023)

The LMS had been at the forefront of pushing diesel technology at least as much as any of the grouped railway companies, having been responsible for the development of the ubiquitous 350hp shunter as well as the first significant express passenger diesels this country had seen (10000-10001).

What the company's late 1940s Chief Mechanical Engineer Henry Ivatt identified was a future need for a medium size class of diesel, ideal for branch line and secondary work. The result was an 827hp (Davey Paxman engine) Bo-Bo, with a cab at one end, complete with duplicate, slave controls to enable it to be driven face-forward in either direction.

The job was contracted to North British Locomotive Co (NBL), Glasgow, who finished 10800 in 1950, thus under British Railways, rather than LMS, rule. Even so, the locomotive still adopted the LMS inspired black and steel livery adopted by its Co-Co forebears.

It was natural that 10800 underwent trials in the Glasgow area, enabling it to be brought back to NBL for snags to be attended to before being sent south. And so it was that Willesden shed was chosen for the Bo-Bo to continue trials.

For a few months in 1952, it worked off Brighton on select South Eastern routes, including to London Victoria (via Oxted).

Plaistow shed on the former London, Tilbury & Southend route was the next home for 10800 from July 1952, again for in-service tests, before returning to the London Midland Region.

BR continued to use the locomotive for another seven years before it succumbed to withdrawal and was stored at Doncaster Works.

Its stay of execution lasted longer… Brush stepped in to buy 10800 for its experimental use in 1962. It duly swapped the Paxman engine out for a Maybach, which drove a Brush AC generator. There was also a new coat of green paint and a name: *Hawk* (albeit never actually chaired on the locomotive).

Tests and trials at Loughborough, as well as the Rugby test plant ensued, together with runs over the former Great Central route. Although a fundamentally sound design, operational niggles forced Brush to finally abandon experiments in 1968. *Hawk* was finally cut five years later.

BR(M) 10100 (BUILT 1950)
In 'OO' form: KR Models (2022)

The first main line diesels commissioned by the LMS (10000-10001) were powered by electric traction, provided by generators coupled to diesel engines. Its next prototype would be diesel-mechanical, although work didn't get underway until the first months of British Railways' rule in 1948.

The 4-8-4 (later 4-4-4-4) was built at Derby under the direction of former Royal Air Force and Rolls-Royce engineer Col Louis Frederick Rudston Fell. Thus 10100 was almost immediately nicknamed the 'Fell'.

His chunky locomotive featured six diesel engines; four driving through a single gearbox and two for driving the various auxiliary machines. Coupled to a common gearbox via 'fluid couplings', each of the four main engines cut-in at different speeds up to, and beyond, 25mph producing the maximum 2,000 hp output.

The engines were mounted in the nose ends, hence the proliferation of air-cooling grilles, while the fluid couplings and gearbox were centrally housed.

After testing on low key, non-passenger trains around Derby and display at Marylebone, the 'Fell' was pressed into front-line service, hauling London – Manchester expresses via the Midland Main Line.

Although the locomotive was highly capable, it was also prone to mechanical problems and was to be seen back at Derby Works more frequently than was desirable, even for a prototype. At the end of a year-long stay there in 1954, it was finally repaired, while also sacrificing its original BR black for green.

Trials over the Settle – Carlisle were successful, and 10100 also continued to run out of St Pancras was reasonable reliability. However, a catastrophic fire at Manchester Central in October 1958 curtailed things and the virtually wrecked 'Fell' was scrapped in 1960.

The Southern Region's trio of 1Co-Co1s have been modelled by Kernow Model Rail Centre for 'OO' gauge. 10201 powers towards Twelve Trees Junction. Mike Wild.

PROTOTYPE DIESELS

Deltic was inherently capable of power outputs seldom achieved

NICK BRODRICK

ENGLISH ELECTRIC DELTIC (BUILT 1955)
In 'OO' form: Bachmann/NRM Exclusive (2008) and Hornby (Expected winter 2024/2025)

The precursor to the 22-strong Class 55s, English Electric's Deltic appeared some eight years before Harold Wilson's landmark 'white heat of technology' speech. With an engine horsepower of 3,300, *Deltic* was inherently capable of power outputs seldom achieved with any British steam locomotive.

This was thanks to EE's previously acquired Napier engine technology, EE afforded its pride and joy twin 1,650hp power units.

Deltic was loaned to British Railways for trials in December 1955, two months after being outshopped from Dick Kerr Works in Preston. It started out running from Liverpool's Edge Hill depot on London expresses until early 1959, with a short spell at Carlisle in 1956 to test its mettle on the gruelling Settle – Carlisle route.

The locomotive's move to Hornsey Depot in north London was a precursor for the duties its successor Vulcan Foundry 'Deltics' would be tasked with. Aside from a couple of platform scraped, *Deltic* proved its 100mph capability. Having proven the concept, it continued in regular East Coast Main Line service between King's Cross and Edinburgh Waverley alongside Gresley 'A4s'.

However, a massive engine failure in March 1961 curtailed *Deltic's* career after 450,000 miles of operation. Happily, the British Transport Commision had the foresight to accession it for the National Collection and was displayed at the Science Museum between 1963 and 1993. Since then, it has resided at the National Railway Museum, York, exhibited in its striking powder blue livery.

BR(S) 10201 – 10203 (BUILT 1950-1954)
In 'OO' form: Kernow Model Centre (2017)

New Zealander Oliver Bulleid, the Southern Railway's flamboyant Chief Mechanical Engineer, will be forever associated with extraordinary designs of locomotives. Think 'Q1', 'Leader' and 'Turf Burner'…

Among those was his passenger diesel locomotive for the newly formed Southern Region of British Railways (albeit ordered by its Southern Railway precursor in 1947). From the exterior, the Ashford, 1950-built 10201 displayed some classic features: Bulleid Firth Brown disc wheels and haunted-looking cab ends, but beneath the skin, it was a remarkably conventional machine – fitted with English Electric 16-cylinder engine. The most unusual aspect, for the time, was the 1Co-Co1 wheel arrangement, which would later form the basis of BR's Class 40 and 'Peaks'.

The Southern diesel was trialled both on home metals as well as between St Pancras and Derby, and was even shown off at the 1951 Festival of Britain on the South Bank in London.

Two more Bulleid diesels followed: 10202 (also Ashford built, 1951) and 10203 (Brighton, 1954). The latter locomotive was superficially the same as its classmates, but was equipped with a souped-up 2,000hp engine – 250hp higher than 10201/2.

In service, the trio were most regularly used on West of England Main Line trains between Waterloo and Exeter, but also featured on the Bournemouth route and the South Eastern section. There were even appearances on the 'Golden Arrow' Pullman to Folkestone/Dover.

By mid-1955 the class, designated 'D16/2' by BR, had all been transferred to Camden shed. The Ashford duo were usually double-headed on the 'Royal Scot', but 10203 was largely restricted to stopping services between Euston and Bletchley.

Livery was, by now, steam locomotive-style Brunswick lined green; it was originally black and silver.

Although reliable, the Bulleid diesels were markedly non-standard and therefore difficult and expensive to maintain. Their inevitable demise finally came to pass in 1963 and all three were cut-up.

ENGLISH ELECTRIC GT3 (BUILT 1961)
In 'OO' form: KR Models (2020)

Perhaps the closest a diesel has ever looked to being a steam locomotive! Built as a 4-6-0, complete with coupled spoked driving wheels and tender (for diesel fuel), the locomotive was the first gas turbine to be equipped with mechanical transmission.

English Electric turned out GT3 from its Vulcan Foundry Works in May 1961 sporting gloss varnished red oxide complete with a BR-esque EE emblem on the tender sides. That was as close to nationalised condition as it ever got, despite the fact that sketch plans later emerged suggesting the prototype would be numbered 19000 and named *Lord of the Isles*.

After being displayed at the Institute of Locomotive Engineers exhibition in Marylebone, GT3 was put through its paces at the Rugby Testing Station. There it was run up to speeds of almost 100mph.

'Road tests' were even more impressive. Its 2,700 (turbine) horsepower propelled it – and its loads of up to 16 coaches – to Shap Summit attaining more than 40mph at the 'top'.

In spite of its undisputed speed and power prowess, GT3's technology was left behind by the British Transport Commission's decision in 1962 to pursue diesel and electric, rather than gas, traction. GT3 was scrapped by Wards of Salford in 1966.

ENGLISH ELECTRIC DP2 (BUILT 1962)
In 'OO' form: Heljan (2012)

It may have looked like a 'Deltic', but comparisons with DP2 are only skin deep. For while this bulky English Electric (Vulcan Foundry) Co-Co shared the same bodyshell, its internals were substantially different. Equipped with a 16CSVT engine (16 being the number of cylinders, C denoting the intercooler, S meaning turbocharged, V was the engine type and T for rail traction), DP2 forged the path that would eventually lead EE to build its highly successful Class 50s.

By the time of its release into trial service in May 1962 on the West Coast Main Line between Euston and Carlisle Citadel/Blackpool Central, BR green has been adopted for prototype locomotives, even if they weren't owned by the company itself. It is therefore telling that DP2 was not adorned with BR emblems.

In summer 1963, the 90mph locomotive was moved to Finsbury Park on the East Coast Main Line and was, unsurprisingly, used on 'Deltic'-type diagrams, unmodified for three years, other than a tweak to the livery from plain Brunswick green to two-tone.

The locomotives was modified by EE with more advanced electric traction parts during 1966 with impressive results; not least its ability to successfully restart a 16-coach train on the 1-in-75 climb to Shap and have it moving at 30mph withing half a mile.

DP2 met a sad end in July 1967 when it collided with a derailed cement train at Thirsk, writing it off, resulting in its scrapping the following year.

PROTOTYPE DIESELS

BRCW D02060 *LION* (BUILT 1962)
In 'OO' form: Heljan (2011)

One of the most extraordinary looking locomotives to ever grace the pre-privatised railway network, *Lion* was a private consortium's hopeful solution for British Rail's Type 4 diesel requirement. The firms – Birmingham Railway Carriage & Wagon Company (BRCW) Sulzer Brothers and Associated Electrical Industries – unveiled their striking off-white with gold trim livery Co-Co in spring 1962 at BRCW's Smethwick Works.

Lion was initially allocated to Wolverhampton Stafford Road to conduct trials, principally on the Western Region's route to Paddington, but it was also memorably entrusted with 16 Mk1 carriages, plus a dynamometer car, over the South Devon Banks.

Teething troubles prevented No. D02060 (its number derived from its works number DEL260) from enjoying a consistent spell in works between September 1961 and April 1963, it was moved to BR's Eastern Region and kept at Finsbury Park depot. It was variably tasked with local commuter trains as well as high-profile dining expresses, such as the 'Master Cutler' and 'Yorkshire Pullman'.

But significant power unit problems in late 1963 dictated an unfruitful visit Doncaster Works before being transferred back to its Birmingham builder for rectification. This never materialised amid a combination of BRCW financial struggles and BR's decision to order production Type 4s (Class 47s) from Brush, Lion was scrapped before end of the year.

CLAYTON-ROLLS ROYCE DHP1 (BUILT 1963)
In 'OO' form: KR Models (Expected winter 2023)

A contender for the most enigmatic prototype is DHP1 – short for Diesel Hydraulic Prototype No. 1 – the little recorded red oxide Bo-Bo of the early 1960s.

Construction began in 1962 under the auspices of Clayton and completed the following year. Although visually similar to the company's Type 1 Class 17 built at the same time, the Type 3 DHP1 was slightly longer and features grills in the nose end, rather than sides.

Unlike the '17', this ultimately rare beast was equipped with four Rolls Royce C8 (375hp) engines (delivering 1,200 hp at the rails), seemingly as an opportunity for the automotive company to demonstrate its potential prowess in the railway industry. This technology was combined with torque converter and gearbox developed for 'Fell' 10100 a decade earlier (see separate entry).

Designed for mixed traffic work, DHP1 was equipped with steam heat equipment. However, its use limited, not helped by the fact that Rolls Royce withdrew from the project in October 1963, just months after the locomotive had been outshopped and only one trial run.

Claytons was left to (successfully) fix problems with the gearbox and further test runs were satisfactory, but with diesel electric power increasingly in favour by the railway, DHP1 was put into store at Clayton's Hatton Works. It did eventually find employment to shunt Derby's Internal Combustion Works, but was scrapped in 1967 at just four years old.

BRUSH HS4000 *KESTREL* (BUILT 1968)
In 'OO' form: Heljan (2009)

It must have been an extraordinary sight, fitting of the era that *Kestrel* was created in. The combination of a curving space-age front end with classically muted browns of the 1960s, Brush's Sulzer engine monster had the power output to match its fierce looks.

Emerging as a late player in the prototype scene, the locomotive boasted an astounding power output of 4,000hp, and was touted as not only having great potential for British main lines, but for the export market too.

Five months into its life, *Kestrel* was hooked up to 20 Mk1s, weighing more than 650 tons, roaring to Shap summit at 46mph. It similarly dismissed its next trials of 32 loaded hoppers (1,600 tons) between Shirebrook and March.

Brush and BR probably never tested the locomotive to its true potential. A laden, 2,028-ton, demonstration train was still well within *Kestrel's* ability, with its driver having to keep the locomotive in a low notch in order to comply with line speed.

However, its Achilles Heel was weight. At 135 tons (operational weight), *Kestrel* was out of bounds for trials on the East Coast Main Line, considered to be a fair speed testbed. The solution in autumn 1969 was to fit modified Class 47 bogies and traction motors, which shaved nine tons from its bulk.

Kestrel proved its worth and outpaced the 'Deltic' timings on King's Cross – Newcastle Central expresses by 14 minutes.

Withdrawal in March 1971 coincided with the locomotive's sale to the USSR state railway, but *Kestrel* seemingly disappeared soon after arriving in the Eastern Bloc that summer.

English Electric gas turbine prototype GT3 leads a mixed rake of Mk 1 and ex-LMS Porthole coaches on Topley Dale. This 4-6-0 has been produced for 'OO' by KR Models. *Mike Wild.*

'FELL' UPGRADES

KR Models' remarkable 'OO' gauge replica of the unique 'Fell' 2-D-2 diesel-electric made its debut in autumn 2022. Using an original British Railways black version, **MIKE WILD** shows how a simple capacitor upgrade can enhance its performance alongside a weathered finish.

Diesel locomotives don't get much more unusual than the 1951-introduced 'Fell' prototype. This experimental locomotive was designed to maximise horsepower while reducing the overall weight using multiple engines. There were six in total – two auxiliaries delivering 150hp each – with the four main engines each producing 500hp making the revolutionary, for the time, locomotive capable of delivering 2,000hp.

In terms of power to weight ratio it was above average in prototype diesel design, but it wasn't without its troubles. Coupling rod bearing failures were common in its original format, which led to the centre section being removed to convert the locomotive to a 2-B-B-2. There were also cooling problems at the trailing end when coupled to trains as well as fuel starvation and troubles with the complex drive system. It was also noisy because of the number of moving components in the drive system.

Despite all this the 'Fell' continued in service until 1958 with most of its main line career spent on the Midland Main Line – it also had a strong association with the Settle – Carlisle line where it underwent load testing. A steam heating boiler fire in 1958 brought the locomotive to the end of its period in service and it was later scrapped at its birthplace of Derby Works in 1960.

KR Models 'OO' gauge model of the 'Fell' was well received on release, but during our testing and operation of the model we found that for absolute reliability with digital sound installed it would benefit from the addition of a stay alive capacitor pack. A stay alive stores energy on board in capacitors and when the decoder detects an interruption in track power supply it draws on the energy stored in the stay alive pack to keep the locomotive moving and the sound on.

As our factory sound fitted model was equipped with an ESU LokSound V5 21-

pin chip, adding a stay alive was a simple process. DCC Concepts produces all the components you need for this including three wire harnesses and an adapter board to convert from the ESU three-wire stay alive system to the two wires of the DCC Concepts Zen Black capacitor pack.

The adapter board and capacitor pack are plug and play components, all you need to do is solder the three wires of the harness to the ESU decoder board and then find space for the new parts.

The tricky part is making the soldered joints on the decoder as the solder pads are very small. We used a fine 1mm nib on our soldering iron, but even so you will need confidence in your soldering abilities for this task.

Having completed the stay alive upgrade, we moved the 'Fell' across our workbench for weathering using a selection of Lifecolor Paints including Frame Dirt from the Rail Weathering set and Burned Black from the Shades of Black set. These were enhanced with Lifecolor Tensocrom Oil and Smoke colours on the underframe and roof respectively to complete the project and make the 'Fell' ready for a return to service.

The following step by step guide explains our project from start to finish and you can read more about the 'Fell' at **www.keymodelworld.com/kr-models**

> "As our factory sound fitted model was equipped with an ESU LokSound V5 21-pin chip, adding a stay alive was a simple process."
>
> **MIKE WILD**

The completed overhaul of the 'Fell' has increased its reliability with the addition of a stay alive capacitor pack while also giving it realistic in-service look.

WHAT WE USED		
PRODUCT	SUPPLIER	CAT NO.
DCC sound fitted 'Fell' 2-D-2	www.krmodels.net	KRM-Fell-OO-S-Black
Zen Black stay alive capacitor	www.dccconcepts.com	DCD-SA3-SS.1
Zen stay alive adapter wires	www.dccconcepts.com	DCD-3WH.3
Lifecolor Rail Weathering acrylics	www.keymodelworld.com/shop	MOD90
Lifecolor Shade of Black acrylics	www.keymodelworld.com/shop	MOD91
Lifecolor Dirty Grease Effect	www.airbrushes.com	UA262
Lifecolor Tensocrom oil	www.airbrushes.com	TSC207
Lifecolor Tensocrom Smoke	www.airbrushes.com	TSC208

WORKBENCH

STEP BY STEP: UPGRADING AND WEATHERING A KR MODELS 'FELL'

1

To remove the body, turn each bogie to the side to access the two screws above it at each end. Use a suitable modelling crosshead screwdriver to release the screws.

2

The first phase of this project is to upgrade this sound fitted 'Fell' with a stay alive capacitor pack from DCC Concepts. We have selected the largest six capacitor pack.

3

The buffers are clip fitted to each end and need to be removed for the body to lift off the chassis. Keep them save for reassembly.

4

Once inside our sound fitted project locomotive, the ESU LokSound V5 chip is mounted on the main Printed Circuit Board with the 28mm round speaker positioned to the rear.

5
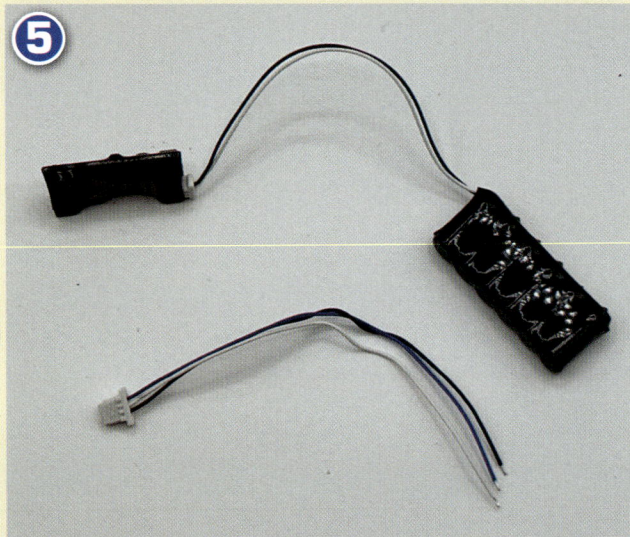
The stay alive pack is designed to be as close to plug and play as possible. The adapter board and stay alive pack are joined together, but we need to solder the three wires of the harness to the ESU sound chip.

6

Start by tinning the left hand three contacts at the rear of the ESU DCC sound decoder. Be very careful when doing this and use the right tool for the job. We used a 1mm nib on our soldering iron.

WORKBENCH

7 The wire ends were tinned with solder as well so that both the wire and the contact point on the decoder are pre-loaded with solder. Heat the two together and arrange the wires as shown here to complete the connection.

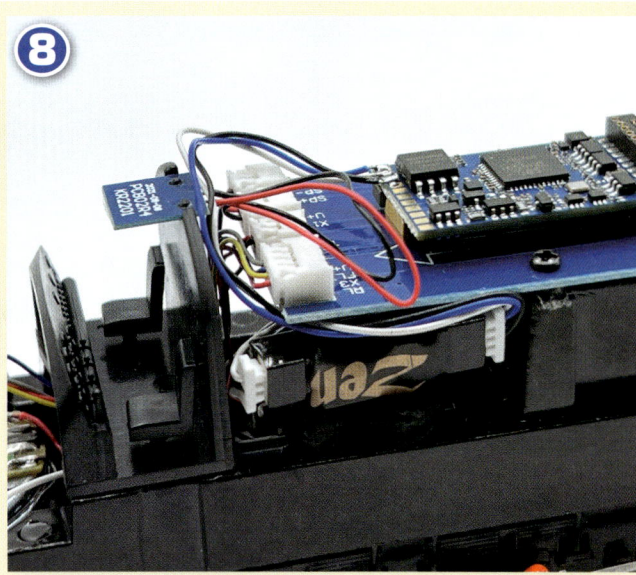

8 The new three-wire harness has now been connected to the adapter board which has been tucked below the main PCB and secured in place with Black Tack.

9 Finding space for the large six capacitor pack was tricky, but we found that it fitted perfect between the cab front bulkhead and the rear of the fan housing above the speaker. To make the installation the cab interior was removed to allow the wires to be routed underneath it.

10 The body has now been refitted in the reverse order of dismantling ensuring that all four buffers and screws are refitted. The model was then tested to check it was working correctly before moving on to the weathering process.

11 The pristine gloss finish of the 'Fell' is smart, but will benefit from light weathering to enhance its detailing. We position each model we weather on a block of wood so that it can be moved without having to handle the locomotive during the process.

12 The starting point is the underframe using Lifecolor Frame Dirt (UA719) from the Rail Weathering set. This is applied using an airbrush with the body masked by holding a business card level with the bottom of the body.

STEP BY STEP: UPGRADING AND WEATHERING A KR MODELS 'FELL'

13 Next the locomotive is inverted to ensure that the lower edges of the underframe all weathered as well as the area above the bogies at each end using the same Frame Dirt colour.

▼ The lower two-thirds of the body are then misted with Frame Dirt from the airbrush ready for the next stage in the process.

14

15 Airbrush cleaner is washed onto the body next to start manipulating the Frame Dirt paint applied to the body to begin creating a realistic finish on the locomotive.

16 Using a cotton bud the Frame Dirt and airbrush cleaner is moved down the body in a vertical motion leaving traces behind around the rivet heads and panel lines. It takes a few minutes to move the paint into the right places, but the effect is very satisfying.

▼ Burned Black is then dusted over the bonnets and windows to simulate dirt build up on the flat surfaces on the locomotive.

17 The roof is tackled next starting with a base layer of Burned Black (UA736) from the Shades of Black Lifecolor set. This is applied by airbrush using a business card as a mask again. By moving the card a couple of millimetres away from the body, a soft edge to the roof colouring can be added.

18

▼ The windows are then cleaned by moistening a cotton bud in a small amount of airbrush cleaner to remove the paint from the glazing.

The underframe of the 'Fell' often appeared coated in oil and grease in images. To replicate this, we used Lifecolor Tensocrom oil sprayed from an airbrush followed by Dirty Grease Effect (UA262) brushed painted onto the red counter weights.

To add detail to the roof Lifecolor Tensocrom Smoke (TSC208) is added around the exhausts from an airbrush. Applying the colours by airbrush allows them to blend into one another.

The buffer heads have had Lifecolor Dirty Grease Effect added to the centres while the main grilles have been blown over with a light coat of Burned Black.

The completed 'Fell' now looks the part of an in-service locomotive. The greave and oil on the underframe over the Frame Dirt base colour highlights the details while the brush application of the Dirty Grease Effect has been done to suggest oil being thrown along the counterweights.

LAYOUT BUILD

DOWNSIZING: BUILDING TWELVEMILL BRIDGE

One year on from the launch of 'TT:120' for the British market by Hornby and Peco we create our first full layout in the new and growing scale. **MIKE WILD** explains the full story of Twelvemill Bridge and its future.

Recent years have seen new gauges appear, with a focus on narrow gauge railways with the growth of 'OO9' and more recently 'O-16.5' through Bachmann, Peco and Dapol. However, 2022 brought a brand-new and unchartered 'standard gauge' scale to the British market – 'TT:120'. This new addition has been spearheaded by track from Peco together with Hornby's entry to 'TT:120' scale in October 2022 with a brand-new range of locomotives, rolling stock, buildings and track accessories. Since then a number of new names have entered to the fold making it more exciting than ever to consider a model railway in this new scale.

'TT:120' has long been part of the European modelling scene, but has never before been available to the British market. In the 1960s Tri-ang dabbled with British outline 'TT' to 3mm scale, but still using 12mm gauge track, and like all British scales was a compromise between scale and gauge – the scale being larger than the track gauge.

The new 'TT:120' products are the first true scale models for the British market where no matter which component you buy for your layout, they are matched in scale with the correct gauge of track to match the trains. The 1:120 scale works out at 2.54mm:1ft with one

Gresley 'A3' 4-6-2 60084 *Trigo* **leads a van train across the five-arch viaduct as Gresley 'A4' 60016** *Silver King* **rushes an express in the opposite direction. The viaduct kit is an exclusive product by PJM Models for the Key Model World Shop.** Jonathan Newton.

LAYOUT BUILD

of its biggest advantages being that a much larger amount of railway can be fitted into a smaller space, but it is also larger than the already established 'N' gauge product range.

As you might expect the initial development of 'TT:120' was limited to a small group of products, but over its first year of availability the range has grown rapidly with much more to come in the next year making it an ideal time to start construction of a new layout.

PLANNING

The overall idea for our layout was simple – to show as many product ranges available for the new scale as possible while creating a realistic setting which could fit into a spare room. The size limit was set at 10ft x 6ft to provide space for a station, goods yards, engine shed, main line double track running plus the intention of a large viaduct scene.

A trackplan was drawn up to combine all the features and at the same time a series of four laser-cut building kits were commissioned from PJM Models to offer unique kits for 'TT:120' scale through the Key Model World Shop. These focused on a viaduct kit based on the Grade II-listed Outwood Viaduct in Radcliffe, Greater Manchester, together with platforms, tunnel portals and a Great Northern Railway signalbox.

For the track we selected Peco's code 55 collection using both the medium and small radius points together with yard lengths of flexible track to generate the most realistic curves possible in the space available.

Planning also required consideration as to how the baseboards would be built and particularly the viaduct scene which would need to be lower than the rest of the layout. In total six 4ft x 2ft boards were assembled using 9mm plywood for the tops supported by a framework of 18mm x 69mm planed timber matching previous baseboards built for *Hornby Magazine* layouts.

The lower boards for the viaduct were set with their tops 144mm lower than the main boards with a separate trackbed being added on timber supports to keep the track

> *The range has grown rapidly with much more to come*
> — MIKE WILD

level throughout. Once complete all of the baseboard surfaces and frames were painted to seal the timber and provide a grey base colour beneath all the layers scenery and ground cover.

TRACK LAYING

When it came to the track for this layout we had two choices: Hornby's sectional track system for the new scale or Peco's collection of fine scale code 55 rail profile products. The Hornby track uses code 80 rail which is a slightly larger profile than the code 55 employed by Peco. The codes refer to the »

rail height – 80 being 80 thousandths of an inch and 55 being 55 thousandths of an inch.

The finer rail profile gives a more realistic look to the finished layout while the use of flexible track means that curves can be flowed to any radius required to meet the layout design. It also means that there will be fewer rail joints around the full circuit, but using flexible track does require a little more work to join it altogether.

If we were to use the Hornby sectional track, every piece comes pre-fitted with metal rail joiners which makes them a simple job to slot together. With flexible track from Peco rail joiners have to be bought separately and then fitted to the ends of each section. On the positive side, the flexible track can be cut to length to suit specific layout designs whereas sectional track restricts layout designs to fixed pieces.

Another big positive for our layout build was the opportunity to use Peco's Unifrog points. These are the latest generation points from Peco which are supplied with the central crossing Vee – the Frog – unpowered. Out of the box they behave like an insulated frog point whereby the vee is unpowered, but long wheelbase locomotives will run through these crossings without any issue. However, short wheelbase locomotives like the Hornby Class 08 would stall on them, but happily the points are pre-fitted with a frog switching wire which can be passed through the baseboard and connected to either a dedicated frog switch or if you are using DCC point motors with a frog switching option this can be used to change the polarity of the frog as the points change. It sounds

Above: The goods yard uses buildings from the Hornby Skaledale range complemented by 3D printed buildings and coal staithes from MS Models. **Mike Wild.**
Below: Modelu 3D printed figures painted by Dan Evason complete the goods yard scene along with road vehicles from Oxford Diecast. **Mike Wild.**

BRAND-NEW VIDEO BUILD SERIES ONLINE NOW!

Visit www.keymodelworld.com/buildingatt120modelrailway to watch our full four-part video series following construction of Twelvemill Bridge. In Part 1 we build the baseboards and platforms, and lay the track to create a working layout ready for the start of scenery, in Part 2 we detail creation of the landscape, Part 3 focuses on ground cover while Part 4 is all about the detail. Part 1 is free to watch on Key Model World and YouTube, Part 2 is free to watch with a Member account on Key Model World and Parts 3 and 4 require a Key Model World Premium Subscription. Visit www.keymodelworld.com/subscribe-today for full details.

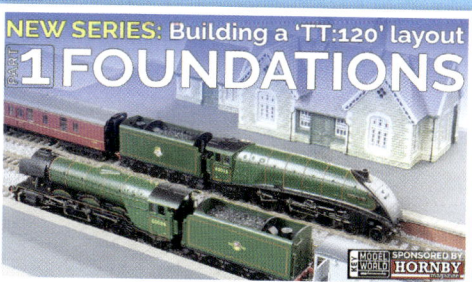
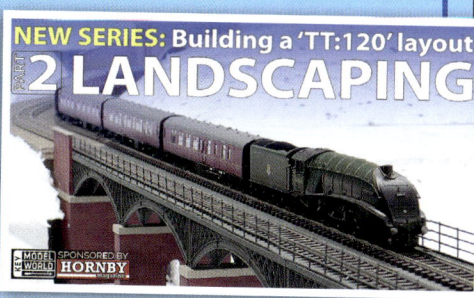
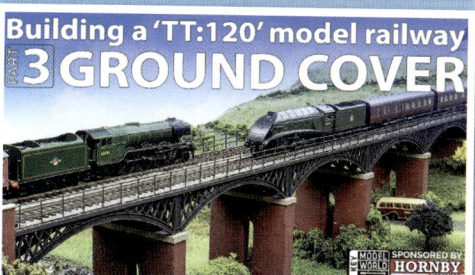
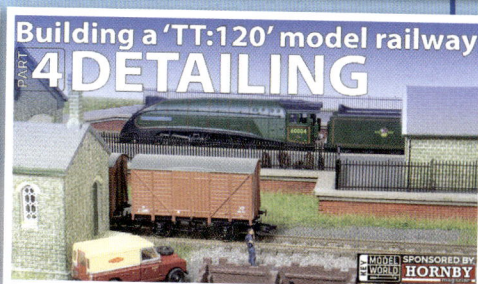

With a rake of Pullmans carriages behind, Gresley 'A4' 60025 *Falcon* speeds through the centre line at Twelvemill Bridge station. The station buildings are from the Hornby Skaledale range. **MIKE WILD.**

'A3' 60084 *Trigo* exits the tunnel with a rake of Mk 1s. The Great Northern Railway tunnel portal is an exclusive kit for the Key Model World Shop by PJM Models. **Mike Wild**.

Falcon steams out of the tunnel on the approach to the station as a goods train disappears into the darkness below the hillside. **Jonathan Newton.**

complicated like that, but once you have done one it will appear much simpler.

The Peco 'TT:120' track range currently consists of medium and short radius points as well as diamond crossings. Plain yard lengths of flexible track are readily available together with matching metal and insulated rail joiners – the latter only really need to be used with analogue control layouts.

In the case of this layout we opted to lay the track direct onto the baseboard rather than using underlay. There were three main reasons for this: first, the smaller track didn't feel like it needed the same ballast shoulder treatment as our 'OO' gauge layouts, so we followed the method used in our 'N' and 'OO9' layouts. Second, once ballasted the noise reducing properties of cork would be reduced significantly, and thirdly, we had a tight timescale to meet for construction of the layout which the cork underlay would add to.

Choices made, we started by laying the plain main lines on the viaduct side of the layout working towards the station scene. Starting with the plain line provided the opportunity to learn how the track responded to curving and pinning which was very similar to Peco's 'N' gauge code 55 track as part of the rail profile is buried in the sleepers. This makes the track strong, but does also mean that it is a little more resistance to bending.

> *"Twelvemill Bridge is now a complete layout, but one which will continue to develop"*
>
> **MIKE WILD**

Swift progress was made around the scene ensuring that when we came to start adding in the points that their location was chosen carefully to avoid baseboard cross members. We also added holes for the point motors and frog wires during track laying so that at the end of the build all points could be operated electrically using DCC Concepts Cobalt IP digital motors.

The most complex part of the track plan was assembling the loops and points through the station. To ensure everything was positioned correctly we built the new laser-cut platform kits from PJM Models ahead of the track laying process and used these to guide installation of the track. The station features three tracks with a loop on the outer circuit against the platform, a central fast line on the outer circuit and a single line through the inner circuit platform. To provide additional train storage, a pair of long sidings were added to the inner circuit which would allow the equivalent of a six-coach train to be stored off the main circuit so that at least four full trains can be on track at any time.

As this is a portable layout each baseboard joint was fitted with a pair of Modeltech Pro-Track Rail Aligners. These are fitted in place of the final three-four sleepers at each baseboard joint and are pinned to the baseboard prior to being soldered to the underside of the rails. Once in place they firmly hold the track in place so that each time Twelvemill Bridge is transported to a show its tracks always align correctly first time.

Completing the track laying phase was addition of wiring using 7/0.2 multi-core equipment wire for the track feeds connected to a twin cable main power bus feed around the layout. The latter links each board together with the track feeds

EXCLUSIVE KITS AVAILABLE NOW!

Key Publishing has partnered with PJM Models to offer a series of brand-new and exclusive laser-cut kits for 'OO' and 'TT:120' scales from the Building a 'TT:120' Model Railway video series. Available now are viaduct kits, platform kits (for 'TT:120' only), Great Northern Railway tunnel portals and, from January, a Great Northern Railway signalbox kit. Visit *www.keymodelworld.com/shop* for full details.

A Replitek telephone box joins the Skaledale station buildings and Oxford Diecast Austin K2 taxi as *Falcon* passes through the centre road. **Mike Wild.**

connecting to the main feed so that all sections are always powered. This method of wiring is simple to complete for digital operation as all red wires join to red wires and all black wires join to black wires by repeating the same circuit repeatedly.

With the layout tested we then weathered the track with Humbrol No. 29 from an aerosol spray can (taking care to cover the point blades with masking tape prior to paint application) after which the track was cleaned and tested again before we moved on to add full ballasting to the layout using Woodland Scenics fine blended grey ballast. This was laid loose, tamped into place with a one-inch paint brush, wetted with a water mister and sealed in place with SBR adhesive for a strong a permanent hold.

LANDSCAPING

The aim of the layout design was to create a scene where it looked like the railway had been carved through the landscape, rather than the other way around – even though that was essentially how the layout would be built.

Polystyrene blocks glued together with PVA glue were used to create the landforms and then shaped with a hot wire foam cutter, working progressively around the scene to blended all the hill shapes together.

The advantage of the dropped board design on the viaduct side of the layout was that the landscape could fall below the level of the railway and then rise above it to suggest a rolling hills scene. The viaduct board called for a multi-level scene with the railway at the top, a road flowing down hill and under the second arch followed by a river at the lowest point passing beneath the fifth arch to create an attractive scene.

After carving the landscape to shape it was overlaid with plaster bandage which was then painted with brown acrylic paint to provide a base colour beneath the ground cover layers which would follow. Next Humbrol Smart Mud was applied to selected areas to represent muddy tracks between fields and in the yard around the farmhouse behind the station. This material is ready to apply direct from pot and adds realistic textures to the ground.

Moving the scene beyond the bare and baren brown scene, Woodland Scenics fine blended green turf was applied and fixed in place with PVA glue prior to layers of Green Scene and Woodland Scenics static grasses through one of its Static Grass King applicators.

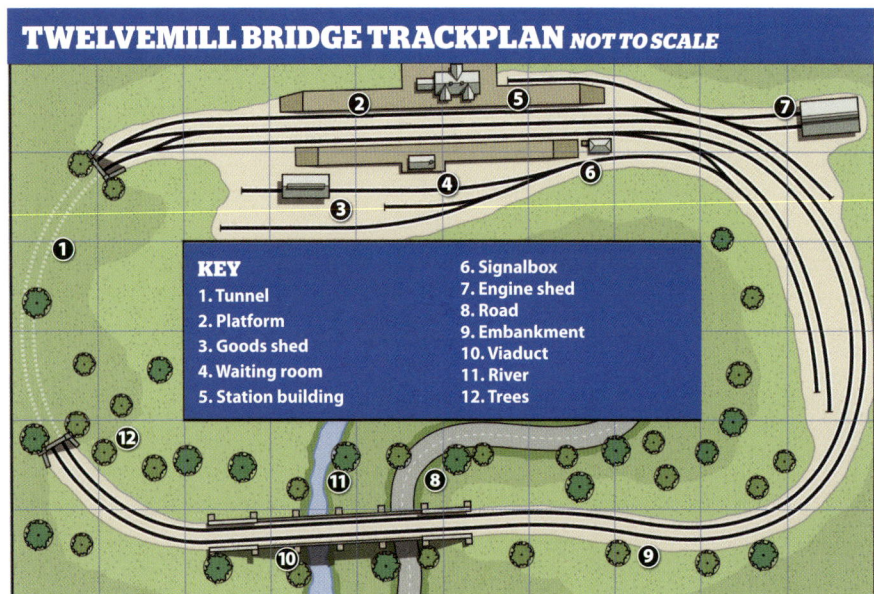

TWELVEMILL BRIDGE TRACKPLAN *NOT TO SCALE*

KEY
1. Tunnel
2. Platform
3. Goods shed
4. Waiting room
5. Station building
6. Signalbox
7. Engine shed
8. Road
9. Embankment
10. Viaduct
11. River
12. Trees

'A4' 60004 *William Whitelaw* crosses the viaduct with a rake of BR Mk 1s recreating a scene from the late 1960s.
Mike Wild.

MS Models 3D printed cottage and barn structures create a small farm house scene with vehicles from Replitek. **Mike Wild.**

Multiple layer of static grass were added followed by coarse and fine turfs from Woodland Scenics paving the way for the addition of hedgerows from Woodland Scenics bushes around the edges of the fields, fine leaf foliage for more overgrown and larger buses around the viaduct scene and a selection of tree and bushes from Primo Models to begin raising interest above the landscape.

ON SHOW

We now had a complete layout ready for its first event appearance at the 2023 *Great Electric Train Show*. Finishing touches were made to the platforms with the addition of fencing by Scale Model Scenery and figures by Dan Evason from the Modelu range. These enhanced the layout significantly which was then stocked with a selection of Gresley 'A3' and 'A4' 4-6-2s from the Hornby 'TT:120' range at the head of BR Mk 1 and Pullman carriages by the same manufacturer. The Key Model World Shop is now an official Hornby TT:120 stockist and you can browse the full range online now at www.keymodelworld.com/shop.

With its Cobalt IP digital point motors changing routes and Hornby Triplex Sound Next18 chips installed in the locomotives, the layout made the most of digital technology, but left the door open for further enhancements after its first show including wiring of the Dapol 'N' gauge signals installed at each end of the station with Train Tech decoder and the addition of lineside signage from West Hill Wagon Works to add a little more detail around the railway.

Twelvemill Bridge is now a complete layout, but one which will continue to develop with the arrival of new products for this enticing new scale. Having had samples of the HST and Class 50 running on the layout at the *Great Electric Train Show*, we can see a bright future for 'TT:120'. 2024 has the promise of the HST, Class 50, Stanier 'Duchess' and many more rolling stock items from Hornby which will make this new scale ever more attractive to modellers.

If you haven't started your railway journey – or maybe you are looking for something new – 'TT:120' is a great choice for a model layout and one which will be easier to fit into the average spare room while creating an impressive scene.

We can't wait to see what is next and will be covering the journey of 'TT:120' in future issues of Hornby Magazine as well as online at www.keymodelworld.com/tt120-model-railways. ∎

Express trains pass in the station which features laser-cut platform kits by PJM Models, Scale Model Scenery fencing and Hornby Skaledale buildings. Mike Wild.

SAS Est.1991

specialauctionservices.com

SAS are the largest model train auctioneers in the country.
Why not get in touch to talk to us about handling your collection?

We are currently consigning for 2024 auctions.
Contact Dominic Foster or Neil Shuttleworth 01635 580595
or Mail@specialauctionservices.com

Special Auction Services, Off Hambridge Lane,
Newbury, Berkshire, RG14 5RL
www.specialauctionservices.com

We are proud to sponsor the Brighton Toy and Model Museum
Members of the Maidenhead Static Model Club

BR/ELECTRO-MOTIVE DIESEL CLASS 66 LOCOMOTIVE
1:76.2 SCALE/OO GAUGE
DUE IN STOCK Q1 2024

Both DC silent (DCC ready) and DCC sound versions are available for all our locomotives.

DC/DCC READY £169.99
DCC SOUND £259.99

Scan the QR Code or visit: www.accurascale.com to view the full range of Class 66 locomotives available to order.

MANUFACTURER OF THE YEAR WINNER 2022 — Hornby Magazine

All models shown are pre-production samples and are subject to refinement and alteration

SHED HEAVEN!

Taking on the Hattons Originals Award Winning Class 66 'Sheds' gave us an excellent platform to build the ultimate Class 66 in 4mm/OO. Our first run consists of six different liveries and numbers whilst updating the tooling in line with the rest of our range. These models will cover all the major and some of the more subtle variations of the class depicting their successful 25 year career.

All Class 66 models feature

- High level of detail
- Die-cast chassis
- Five-pole motor with twin flywheels
- DCC ready & DCC sound (ESU loksound v5) options
- Details specific to individual prototypes
- High fidelity metal and plastic parts
- Rotating axle boxes
- Helical gears for maximum performance
- Comprehensive lighting functions
- Enhancing the model with redesigned axle boxes for the smoothest running
- Easier decoder access with a lift off roof section upgrading the PCB to eliminate wiring
- Revised lighting to give access to day, night and yard mode under DCC
- Hall sensors added to DCC sound models
- Cab access step and handrails have been moved from body mount to chassis mount to allow for breakage free access to chassis
- Cab Front Handrails now have the option of 5 point or 7 point mounting with correct round profile handrail mounts
- And other typical Accurascale features.

www.accurascale.com

Brand-new for 'OO' gauge through EFE Rail are the Southern Region Bulleid Raworth 'Booster' Co-Co electrics. These new locomotives are due for release in December 2023 with two samples seen here passing on the *Hornby Magazine* test track. **MIKE WILD.**

Forward to 2024

New scales, new announcements and unexpected locomotives make up the 250 new products planned by model manufacturers. **MIKE WILD** looks ahead to 2024 and beyond in our annual survey.

FORWARD TO 2024

Rapido Trains UK has been increasing its list of new locomotive projects with an impressive 12 planned for 'OO' gauge including the USATC 'S160' 2-8-0 and Manning Wardle 'L' 0-6-0ST. These are CAD renders for the new locomotive models. **Rapido Trains UK.**

The collection of ready-to-run locomotives, carriages and wagons on offer continues to become an ever more comprehensive collection, and with an increasing number of locomotives which would once have been unthinkable.

In this year's survey we are listing 251 new models and for the first time we are covering 'TT:120' scale products with a listing of all the confirmed products with release dates from Hornby so far. The survey covers 'OO', 'O', 'N', 'OO9' and 'TT:120' scales with 'O-16.5' being omitted this year following release of the Lionheart Lynton and Barnstaple Manning Wardle 2-6-2T and carriages in October 2023.

'OO' gauge remains the busiest section of the model railway scene with an impressive 110 items in the survey followed by 'O' gauge (49 items), 'TT:120' (45), 'N' gauge (42) then 'OO9' (4). And there are products which have been announced and delivered between our annual surveys which have never entered the listings including the Mainline Hunslet, refurbished 4-CEP units and more from Bachmann.

'OO' GAUGE

The pace of new model announcements for 'OO' gauge seems to have no limits and there are now more manufacturers than ever before creating locomotives and rolling stock for the scale.

Rapido Trains UK has been prolific in adding new steam engines to its collection with its most recent announcements in early November including the addition of four further locomotives with a broad range of subjects including South Eastern and Chatham Railway, Metropolitan Railway, industrial locomotives and more.

Unique and unusual locomotives continue to be a common theme in 'OO' gauge, with KR Models, Heljan and Hornby picking these subjects for new releases. One of the most surprising, but equally enticing, is Hornby's plan for a Hornby Dublo inspired model of the prototype 'Deltic' which is set to feature a die-cast body as part of its impressive specification.

An influx of new features have come through with new releases with Accurascale leading the charge with factory sound installations while Hornby has looked to enhance its steam locomotives with the addition of firebox flicker, working locomotive lamps on selected engines as well as introducing touch switching for the taillamp on the tender of the recently released LMS 'Turbomotive' 4-6-2.

The balance between steam and diesel has moved in favour of the latter, and with some significant locomotive classes being restarted afresh including the Class 31, 50, 60 and 66. Modern multiple units have also been selected for development with Revolution Trains focusing on the Class 175 and 180 DMUs.

Rolling stock options continue to expand and again Rapido Trains has been busy producing new steam era wagons while Accurascale has selected the BR 16ton mineral wagons to grow its 'Powering Britain' collection as well as the NER 20ton coal hoppers.

Modern era modellers have a huge selection of new wagons in development for a wide variety of traffic types including steel coils, scrap, engineering, cars, car parts, timber and more.

Passenger rolling stock is a little more limited at present, but there are still the LNER 'Coronation' carriages to look forward to from Hornby in 2024

Locomotion Models, Rails of Sheffield and Bachmann have joined forces to create a ready-to-run model of prototype HST power car 41001 for 'OO' gauge. It is expected to arrive in 2024. **Bachmann.**

together with BR Mk 1 57ft suburbans and Mk 2b/c carriages from Accurascale as well as GWR Autocoach and Inspection Saloon vehicles from Dapol.

For the full list of 'OO' gauge ready-to-run projects see Table 1 and Table 2.

from Lionheart Trains to build on the '45XX' released during 2023.

Ellis Clark Trains Stanier 'Black Five' is in the final phase of production for release in late 2023-early 2024 while the same manufacturer has now received the first engineering samples of its collection of Pullman K-Type carriages which expected to available in 2024 to expand the range of passenger vehicles available to the scale.

Goods rolling stock has expanded beyond the traditional steam era focus of 'O' gauge with Dapol producing the HIA bogie hoppers alongside development of its Class 66 while Ellis Clark Trains is continuing work on its Sealion and Seacow ballast hoppers together with the Shark ballast plough. Steam era wagons haven't been left out though with Dapol growing its range of four-wheel wagons including the BR 14ton slope sided mineral wagon and BR 24ton iron ore hopper.

See Tables 3 and 4 for the full list of 'O' gauge locomotive and rolling stock projects.

Dapol has revised the CAD drawings, drive system and electronics in its long-awaited new Bulleid 'Light Pacific' for 'N' gauge. This is the latest drawing for the model which is now set to move forward to tooling. Dapol.

'O' GAUGE

The largest of the ready-to-run scale in our survey has plenty to look forward to in 2024 including all-new versions of the Class 37/0 and Class 45 from Heljan together with the long-awaited Class 117 DMUs which are expected in early 2024.

While big locomotives continue to remain popular, both the Ruston 48DS and 88DS are being offered for 'O' gauge with Heljan and Accurascale respectively. The Accurascale 88DS is its first ready-to-run locomotive for 'O' gauge which is set for release in 2024.

Steam motive power is being developed by Minerva Models, including the USA 0-6-0T, while Dapol and its Lionheart Trains arm are continuing development of the Hunslet 'Austerity' 0-6-0ST and BR '3MT' 2-6-2T. A new entry this year is the GWR '4575' 2-6-2T

'N' GAUGE

The smallest British scale has support from Bachmann's Graham Farish brand together with Dapol, Revolution Trains and Rapido Trains UK which has created a list of more than 40 items for release in 'N' gauge. Impressively one name is leading the charge in 'N' gauge – Revolution Trains – with 23 of the 42 products planned for the scale in development with the brand.

Highlights of the current project list include the all-new Bulleid 'Light Pacifics' from Dapol which has now reached the end of the CAD drawing stage with confirmation of a new chassis design including a coreless motor and a choice of DCC ready, DCC fitted and DCC sound fitted versions. Revolution Trains is pushing forward with its ground-breaking London Underground 1938 tube train for »

TABLE 1 – 'OO' GAUGE NEW LOCOMOTIVE PROJECTS 2024 FORWARDS			
PRODUCT	REGION	MANUFACTURER	EXPECTED
Highland Railway 'Jones Goods' 4-6-0	Scottish	Rapido Trains UK	2024
Metropolitan 'E' 0-4-4T	Metropolitan Line	Rapido Trains UK	2024
GWR steam railmotor	Western	Kernow MRC	2024
GWR '28XX'/'2884' 2-8-0	Western	Dapol	2025
GWR '43XX' 2-6-0 (new variants)	Western	Dapol	2024
GWR '44XX' 2-6-2T	Western	Rapido Trains UK	2024
LBSCR 'E1' 0-6-0T	Southern	Rapido Trains UK	2024
SECR 'O1' 0-6-0	Southern	Rapido Trains UK	2024
SR Bulleid 'Leader' 0-6-0+0-6-0	Southern	KR Models	2024
MR 'Big Bertha' 0-10-0 2290/58100	Midland	KR Models	2024
LMS 'Black Five' 4-6-0	Midland	Hornby	2024
GNR Stirling Single 4-2-2 with small tender	Eastern	Rapido Trains UK	2024
LNER 'B17/5' 4-6-0	Eastern	Hornby	2024
NER 'J26' 0-6-0	Eastern	Oxford Rail	TBC
LNER 'J52/2' 0-6-0ST	Eastern	Rapido Trains UK	2024
LNER 'J67'-'J69' 0-6-0Ts	Eastern	Accurascale	2024
LNER 'P2' 2-8-2 (2007/steam gen)	Eastern	Hornby	2024
LNER 'Y7' 0-4-0T	Eastern	Rapido Trains UK	2024
USATC 'S160' 2-8-0	Western/Southern	Rapido Trains UK	2025
Port of Par Bagnall 0-4-0ST	Industrial	Rapido Trains UK	2024
Hawthorn Leslie 0-4-0ST	Industrial	Dapol	2024
Haydock Foundry 0-6-0WT	Industrial	KR Models	2024
Manning Wardle 'L' 0-6-0ST	Industrial	Rapido Trains UK	2025
DHP1 prototype Bo-Bo	Midland	KR Models	2024
Hunslet 1,124hp Bo-Bo diesel	Industrial	KR Models	2023
Met-Vic 18100 gas turbine	Western	Rails/Heljan	2023
Met-Vic E1000/E2001 25kV electric	Midland	Rails/Heljan	2023
Prototype 'Deltic' Co-Co	Eastern/Midland	Hornby	2024
Ruston & Hornsby 88DS 0-4-0	Various	Hornby	2023
Class 02 0-4-0	Various	Heljan	2023
Class 04 Drewry 0-6-0 diesel shunter	Eastern/Southern	Rapido Trains UK	TBA
Class 18 Clayton CBD90 Bo-Bo	Industrial	Revolution Trains	2024
Class 25/1 Bo-Bo	Various	Bachmann	2024
Class 25/2 Bo-Bo	Various	Bachmann	2024
Class 25/2 and 25/3 Bo-Bos	Various	SLW	2024
Class 26 (new tooling) Bo-Bo	Scottish	Heljan	2024
Class 31 A1A-A1A	Various	Accurascale	2024
Class 40 1Co-Co1	Midland/Eastern	KR Models	2024
Class 41 prototype HST power car	Western	Rails/Locomotion/Bachmann	2024
Class 47 Co-Co	Various	Heljan	2023
Class 50 Co-Co	Midland/Western	Accurascale	2024
Class 56 Co-Co	Midland/Eastern	Cavalex Models	2023
Class 60 Co-Co	Various	Cavalex Models	2024
Class 66 Co-Co	All	Accurascale	2024
Class 69 Co-Co	Various	Bachmann	TBA
Class 86/2 Bo-Bo electric	Midland/Eastern	Heljan	2024
Class 88 Bo-Bo electro-diesel	Midland/Scottish	Rails/Dapol	2024
Class 89 Co-Co electric	Eastern	Rails/Accurascale	2024
Class 93 tri-mode Bo-Bo	Rail Ops Group	Revolution Trains	2024
Class 104 two- and three-car DMU	Midland/Scotland	Heljan	2024
Class 142 two-car DMU	Midland/Eastern	Realtrack	2024
Class 175 two-car DMU	Midland/Wales	Revolution Trains	2024
Class 175 three-car DMU	Midland/Wales	Revolution Trains	2024
Class 180 five-car DMU	Various	Revolution Trains	2024
Class 755/3 three-car Bi-MU	Great Eastern	Hornby	2024
Class 755/4 four-car Bi-MU	Great Eastern	Hornby	2024
SR Bulleid Raworth 'Booster' Co-Co electrics	Southern	EFE Rail	2023
4-DD four-car EMU	Southern	KR Models	2024
TOTAL: 58 STEAM: 23 DIESEL/ELECTRIC: 35			

In 'TT:120' scale Hornby is making rapid strides through development of its Class 50 model. These are the first factory decorated samples. Jonathan Newton.

'N' gauge with first engineering samples being received in time for display at the 2023 Great Electric Train Show. There is also a race to the finish with all-new Class 59s being developed by both Dapol and Revolution Trains for 'N' gauge.

Incoming rolling stock includes the Mk 5a Transpennine Express sets through Revolution following delivery of the Caledonian Sleeper Mk 5s in September. The new Pullmans are also in progress while a string of freight vehicles are being developed including Cartic-4s for 'N' as well as steam era iron ore hoppers, modern engineering wagons and more.

See Tables 5 and 6 for the full list of 'N' gauge locomotive and rolling stock projects.

NARROW GAUGE

The narrow gauge market has slowed at little at present following a flurry of releases from Bachmann on the Mainline Hunslet including the original Penrhyn Quarry 0-4-0STs and the rebuilding of them for the Ffestiniog Railway as both 0-4-0STT and 2-4-0STT locomotives.

However, there are still exciting new locomotives to look forward to including the Baguley Drewry 4wDM shunter which, while humble in its appearance, will make a superb addition to any narrow gauge layout. Peco has also promised the 'Large England' 0-4-0STT as the follow up to its hugely popular 'Small England' 0-4-0STT for release in 2024.

There are currently just two rolling stock projects on the cards for 'OO9' – the Ashover Light Railway carriage from Bachmann and the Ffestiniog Railway Bowsider coaches from Peco, but we are hoping to see further announcements in 2024 for this scale.

See Table 7 for the full list of 'OO9' gauge model projects.

'TT:120' SCALE

Brand-new to the British market in 2022 was 'TT:120' scale. This new choice for model railways received a big boost in October 2022 when Hornby announced a significant range of new locomotive and rolling stock

Accurascale has taken over the Hatton's Class 66 tooling and is working through a full overhaul to bring out a new collection of models in early 2024. Amongst the first releases is last-built Class 66 66779 Evening Star seen here as a decorated running sample on the *Hornby Magazine* test track. Mike Wild.

items for progressive release. One year on and three locomotives, two sets of carriages and six wagons have all been released to allow modellers to make a start in this attractive scale.

The confirmed list of products with definite delivery dates is shorter than the wider plan, but in this survey we have focused on the locomotive and rolling stock model which have been confirmed for release. These are the Stanier 'Duchess' 4-6-2, Class 43 HST power cars, Class 50 and Class 66. However, Hornby has also put out plans in principle to produce a much larger number of locomotives including the BR '9F' 2-10-0, GWR 'Castle' 4-6-0, LMS 'Black Five' 4-6-0 and BR 'Britannia' 4-6-2 on the steam front together with classes 31, 37, 47, 60, 67, 73 and 800 for diesel and electric models.

The next rolling stock releases will be the Stanier 57ft Period III carriages to be followed in 2024 by BR Mk 2F and Mk 3 vehicles plus 21ton mineral wagons, HAA coal hoppers, TTA 45ton tankers and more for freight modellers.

Even after just one year, the future of 'TT:120' is looking bright, particularly has Hornby has opened out availability of its new range of products to a selected number of retailers to »

TABLE 2 – 'OO' GAUGE NEW ROLLING STOCK PROJECTS 2023 FORWARDS

PRODUCT	REGION	MANUFACTURER	EXPECTED
GWR Diagram N Autocoach	GWR	Dapol	2024
GWR Q13 Inspection Saloon	Western	Dapol	2024
GWR 'B-set' carriages	Western	Rapido Trains UK	2024
LNER 'Coronation' Brake /Kitchen Third	LNER	Hornby	2024
LNER 'Coronation' Double Open First	LNER	Hornby	2024
LNER 'Coronation' Open/Kitchen Third	LNER	Hornby	2024
LNER 'Coronation' Open/Brake Third	LNER	Hornby	2024
LNER 'Coronation' Observation Car	LNER	Hornby	2024
LNER Quad-Art articulated carriages	LNER	Ellis Clark Trains	2024
BR Newton Chambers car carriers	Eastern	EFE Rail	2023
BR Mk 1 57ft suburban Brake Second	Various	Accurascale	2023
BR Mk 1 57ft suburban Composite	Various	Accurascale	2023
BR Mk 1 57ft suburban Second Open	Various	Accurascale	2023
BR Mk 1 57ft suburban Composite Lavatory	Various	Accurascale	2023
BR Mk 1 57ft suburban Second Lavatory Open	Various	Accurascale	2023
BR Mk 1 57ft suburban Second	Various	Accurascale	2023
BR Mk 2b Brake Corridor First	Various	Accurascale	2023
BR Mk 2b Corridor First/Corridor Second	Various	Accurascale	2023
BR Mk 2b Tourist Second Open	Various	Accurascale	2023
GWR Class 802/1 four-coach pack	Western	Hornby	2024
LNER Class 801/2 four-coach pack	Eastern	Hornby	2024
Ex-Wisbech and Upwell Tramcar	Film	Rapido Trains UK	2024
1907 RCH open wagons	Various	Rapido Trains UK	2024
LNWR Diagram 88 box vans	LNWR	Rapido Trains UK	2024
GWR Y4 banana van	Western	Rapido Trains UK	2024
GWR MICA B insulated van	Western	KR Models	2024
GWR 'Macaw B' bogie bolster wagon	Western	Hornby	2024
SR banana van (Dia. 1478)	Southern	Accurascale	2023
SR banana van (Dia. 1479)	Southern	Accurascale	2023
LMS/LNER Lowmac wagon	Various	Rapido Trains UK	2024
LMS Salmon bogie wagon	Various	Hornby	2024
NER/LNER 20ton coal hoppers	Eastern	Accurascale	2024
Class A/Class B 14ton tanker	Various	Dapol	2024
BR 16ton mineral wagons	Various	Accurascale	2024
BR Borail B bogie wagon	Various	Revolution Trains	2024
BR Borail C bogie wagon	Various	Revolution Trains	2024
BR 'Mullet' bogie wagon	Various	Revolution Trains	2024
BR YQA 'Parr' bogie wagon	Various	Revolution Trains	2024
BR YQA 'Super Tench' wagon	Various	Revolution Trains	2024
BR Cartic-4 car carriers	Various	Revolution Trains	2024
BIA/BWA/BXA/BZA covered steel carrier	Various	Cavalex Models	TBC
Cowans Sheldon 15ton crane	Various	Oxford Rail	TBC
HOA hopper wagon	Various	Revolution Trains	2023
IHA bogie steel wagon	Various	Revolution Trains	2024
JGA/PHA bogie aggregate wagon	Various	Cavalex Models	2023
JHA bogie aggregate hopper	Western	Dapol	2024
KSA Rover Cube wagons	Various	Revolution Trains	2024
KSA timber carriers	Various	Revolution Trains	2024
OAA open wagon	Various	Rapido Trains UK	2023
PCA alumina tanks	Scottish	Revolution Trains	2024
PHA/JYA bogie aggregate box wagons	Western	Cavalex Models	2024
PXA steel coil wagons	Various	Rails/Cavalex Models	2024
JXA steel scrap wagons	Various	Rails/Cavalex Models	2024
TTA 45ton tanker	Various	Hornby	2024
Torpedo ore wagon	Industrial	KR Models	2023
TOTAL: 53			

TABLE 3 – 'O' GAUGE NEW LOCOMOTIVE PROJECTS 2023 FORWARDS

PRODUCT	REGION	MANUFACTURER	EXPECTED
GWR '56XX' 0-6-2T	Western	Minerva Models	2024
GWR '4575' 2-6-2T	Western	Lionheart Trains	2025
SR 'USA' 0-6-0T	Southern	Minerva Models	2024
LMS 'Black Five' 4-6-0	Midland	Ellis Clark/Darstaed	2023
LNER 'J70' 0-6-0T	Eastern	Rapido Trains UK	TBA
LNER 'J94' 0-6-0ST	Eastern/Industrial	Dapol	2024
BR '3MT' 2-6-2T	Various	Lionheart Trains	2024
Class 02 0-4-0 shunter	Various	Heljan	2024
Class 09 0-6-0 shunter	Southern	Gaugemaster/Dapol	TBA
Class 37/0 (split headcodes) Co-Co	Various	Heljan	2024
Class 37/0 (centre headcodes) Co-Co	Various	Heljan	2024
Class 45 1Co-Co1 (sealed beam headlights)	Midland/Eastern	Heljan	2024
Class 66 Co-Co	All	Dapol	TBC
Class 117 three-car DMU	Western/Midland	Heljan	2024
Class 121 single-car DMU	Western/Midland	Heljan	2024
Class 122 single-car DMU	Western/Midland	Heljan	2024
Class 149 trailer car	Western/Midland	Heljan	2024
Class 150 trailer car	Western/Midland	Heljan	2024
Class 153 single-car DMU	Various	Heljan	2024
Ruston Hornsby 48DS 4wDM	Industrial	Heljan	2024
Ruston Hornsby 88DS 4wDM	Industrial	Accurascale	2024
TOTAL: 21 STEAM: 7 DIESEL: 14			

TABLE 4 – 'O' GAUGE NEW ROLLING STOCK PROJECTS 2023 FORWARDS

VEHICLE	REGION	MANUFACTURER	EXPECTED
LMS 50ft Inspection Saloon	Various	Heljan	2024
SR Bulleid semi-open Brake Corridor Third/Second	Southern	Greenwood and Pring	2024
SR Bulleid Corridor Composite	Southern	Greenwood and Pring	2024
SR Bulleid Open Third/Second	Southern	Greenwood and Pring	2024
SR Bulleid Restaurant First Open	Southern	Greenwood and Pring	2024
SR Bulleid Restaurant Kitchen Third	Southern	Greenwood and Pring	2024
Pullman K Type Brake Parlour Third	Various	Ellis Clark/Darstaed	2024
Pullman K Type Parlour First	Various	Ellis Clark/Darstaed	2024
Pullman K Type Parlour Third	Various	Ellis Clark/Darstaed	2024
Pullman K Type Kitchen First	Various	Ellis Clark/Darstaed	2024
Pullman K Type Kitchen Third	Various	Ellis Clark/Darstaed	2024
BR Mk 1 BCK	All	Lionheart Trains	2024
BR Mk 2 FK	All	Heljan	2024
BR Mk 2 TSO	All	Heljan	2024
BR Mk 2 BSO	All	Heljan	2024
BR Mk 2 BFK	All	Heljan	2024
SR CCT/PMV four-wheel parcels van	Various	Heljan	2024
GWR N32 'Felix Pole' coal wagon	Western	Minerva Models	2024
GWR 'Toad' brake van	Western	Dapol	2024
BR 14ton slope sided mineral wagon	Various	Dapol	2024
BR 24ton iron ore hopper	Various	Dapol	2024
HIA bogie aggregates hopper	Various	Dapol	2024
YGB 'Sealion' ballast hopper	Various	Ellis Clark Trains	2024
YGB 'Seacow' ballast hopper	Various	Ellis Clark Trains	2024
ZJV 'Mermaid' ballast tippler	Various	Flangeway/Dapol	2025
ZUA 'Shark' ballast plough	Various	Ellis Clark Trains	2024
ZZA snowplough	Various	Flangeway/Dapol	2024
TOTAL: 28			

In 'OO9' Bachmann is working on its Baguley Drewery 4wDM for narrow gauge modellers with release expected in 2024. **Bachmann.**

Revolution Trains Class 313 units for 'N' gauge are progressing towards delivery following receipt of factory painted samples in mid-2023. **Revolution Trains.**

In 'O' gauge Dapol's Hunslet 'Austerity' 0-6-0ST is approaching completion. This is one of the decorated samples for the new model. **Dapol.**

Southern Region electric modellers will be delighted to see the KR Models 4DD arrive in 2024 for 'OO'. **Mark Chivers.**

increase availability. In addition there are many suppliers offering accessories, buildings and details to enhance a layout which we have shown in our latest layout build (see pages 106-115).

THE FUTURE

Even as we assemble this survey there are new products in the planning for announcement, particularly with the Warley National Model Railway Exhibition coming up at the end of November 2023 – a time when traditionally there are a number of new product announcements. Then there is the Hornby 2024 catalogue launch in January and by the time you read this the Southern Region Bulleid Raworth electrics from EFE Rail should be about to arrive in the shops.

The model railway hobby is as busy and vibrant as ever and with the introduction of more ready-to-run rolling stock for 'OO9' and the growth of 'TT:120' over its first year it only serves to offer us all a greater choice of models to add to our collection. Could it be any better? ■

The unique Class 89 is expected to arrive in the first quarter of 2024 with Accurascale and Rails of Sheffield. **Accurascale.**

Above: Eastern Region steam modellers are being treated to the 'J67'-'J69' 0-6-0T family in 'OO' gauge by Accurascale. These are the engineering samples for the new locomotives which are planned for release in 2024. **Accurascale.**

TABLE 5 – 'N' GAUGE NEW LOCOMOTIVE PROJECTS 2023 FORWARDS

VEHICLE	REGION	MANUFACTURER	EXPECTED
GWR 'Large Prairie' 2-6-2T	Western	Sonic Models	2023
GWR '63XX' 2-6-0	Western	Dapol	2024
SR air-smoothed 'West Country' 4-6-2	Southern	Dapol	2024
SR rebuilt 'West Country' 4-6-2	Southern	Dapol	2024
Class 44 1Co-Co1	Midland	Rapido Trains UK	2024
Class 45 1Co-Co1	Midland/Eastern	Rapido Trains UK	TBA
Class 46 1Co-Co1	Various	Rapido Trains UK	TBA
Class 59 Co-Co diesel	Western/Eastern	Dapol	2024
Class 59 Co-Co diesel	Western/Eastern	Revolution Trains	2024
Class 69 Co-Co diesel	Various	Graham Farish	TBA
Class 87 Bo-Bo electric	Midland	Dapol	2024
Class 120 Swindon cross-country DMU	Western	Revolution Trains	TBA
Class 158 two-car DMU	Various	Graham Farish	2023
Class 175 two-car DMU	Midlands/Wales	Revolution Trains	TBC
Class 175 three car DMU	Midlands/Wales	Revolution Trains	TBC
Class 180 five-car DMU	Various	Revolution Trains	TBC
Class 313/314 EMU	Various	Revolution Trains	2023
Class 377 Electrostar EMU	Western/Southern	Revolution Trains	TBA
Class 450 EMU	Southern	Graham Farish	2024
LT 1938 tube stock	London	Revolution Trains	2024

TOTAL: 20 STEAM: 4 DIESEL/ELECTRIC: 16

TABLE 6 – 'N' GAUGE NEW ROLLING STOCK PROJECTS 2023 FORWARDS

VEHICLE	REGION	MANUFACTURER	EXPECTED
SR GM Inspection Saloon/Caroline	Southern	Revolution Trains	2023
Pullman K Type all-steel Brake Parlour Third	Various	Revolution Trains	2023
Pullman K Type all-steel Parlour First	Various	Revolution Trains	2023
Pullman K Type all-steel Parlour Third	Various	Revolution Trains	2023
Pullman K Type all-steel Kitchen First	Various	Revolution Trains	2023
Pullman K Type all-steel Kitchen Third	Various	Revolution Trains	2023
LNER Dynamometer car	Eastern	Rapido Trains UK	2024
BR Newton Chambers car carriers	Eastern	Sonic Models	2024
Trans Pennine Mk 5 carriage sets	Midland/Eastern	Revolution Trains	2024
BR 24.5ton iron ore hoppers	Midland/Eastern	Revolution Trains	TBA
BR Borail B bogie wagon	Various	Revolution Trains	2024
BR Borail C bogie wagon	Various	Revolution Trains	2024
BR 'Mullet' bogie wagon	Various	Revolution Trains	2024
BR YQA 'Parr' bogie wagon	Various	Revolution Trains	2024
BR YQA 'Super Tench' wagon	Various	Revolution Trains	2024
Cartic-4 car carriers	Various	Revolution Trains	2024
FNA-D Nuclear flask carrier	Various	Revolution Trains	2024
FSA/FTA Freightliner container flats	Various	C=Rail	2024
O&K 102ton JHA hopper wagons	Western	Dapol	2024
OAA air-braked open wagon	Various	Rapido Trains UK	2024
PTA/JTA bogie tippler wagons	Various	Revolution Trains	TBA
VIX Ferry van	Various	N Gauge Society	TBA

TOTAL: 22

TABLE 7 – 'OO9' GAUGE NEW PROJECTS 2023 FORWARDS

VEHICLE	REGION	MANUFACTURER	EXPECTED
Baguley-Drewry 4wDM	Industrial	Bachmann	2024
FR 'Large England' 0-4-0STT	Ffestiniog	Peco	2024
Ashover Light Railway carriage	Narrow gauge	Bachmann	TBA
FR 'Bowsider' coach	Ffestiniog	Peco	2023

TOTAL: 4

TABLE 8 – 'TT:120' SCALE NEW LOCOMOTIVES 2024 FORWARDS

VEHICLE	REGION	MANUFACTURER	EXPECTED
GWR '57XX' 0-6-0PT	Western	Hornby	TBC
GWR 'Castle' 4-6-0	Western	Hornby	TBC
LMS 'Princess Coronation' 4-6-2	Midland	Hornby	2024
LMS 'Black Five' 4-6-0	Midland	Hornby	TBC
BR 'Britannia' 4-6-2	Various	Hornby	TBC
BR '9F' 2-10-0	Various	Hornby	TBC
BR Class 31 A1A-A1A diesel	Various	Hornby	TBC
BR Class 37 Co-Co diesel	Various	Hornby	TBC
BR Class 43 HST power cars	Various	Hornby	2024
BR Class 47 Co-Co diesel	Various	Hornby	TBC
BR Class 50 Co-Co diesel	Various	Hornby	2024
Class 66 Co-Co diesel	Various	Hornby	2024
Class 67 Bo-Bo diesel	Various	Hornby	TBC
BR Class 73 Bo-Bo electro-diesel	Southern	Hornby	TBC
Class 800 InterCity Express Train	Various	Hornby	TBC

TOTAL: 16 STEAM: 6 DIESEL/ELECTRIC: 10

Hornby's Class 755 Flirt unit family has reached the running sample stage.

TABLE 9 – 'TT:120' SCALE NEW ROLLING STOCK PROJECTS 2023 FORWARDS

VEHICLE	REGION	MANUFACTURER	EXPECTED
GWR Collett bow-end Brake Third	Western	Hornby	TBC
GWR Collett bow-end Corridor Composite	Western	Hornby	TBC
LNER Gresley Corridor Composite	Eastern	Hornby	TBC
LNER Gresley Corridor Brake Third	Eastern	Hornby	TBC
LMS 50ft Passenger Brake	Midland	Hornby	2023
LMS 57ft Corridor First	Midland	Hornby	2023
LMS 57ft Corridor Third	Midland	Hornby	2023
LMS 57ft Brake Third	Midland	Hornby	2023
BR Mk 2e Brake Standard Open	Various	Hornby	2024
BR Mk 2e First Open	Various	Hornby	2024
BR Mk 2e Tourist Standard Open	Various	Hornby	2024
BR Mk 2f Brake Standard Open	Various	Hornby	2024
BR Mk 2f First Open	Various	Hornby	2024
BR Mk 2f Tourist Standard Open	Various	Hornby	2024
BR Mk 3 Trailer Restaurant Buffet	Various	Hornby	2024
BR Mk 3 Trailer First Open	Various	Hornby	2024
BR Mk 3 Trailer Standard Open	Various	Hornby	2024
BR Mk 3 Trailer Guard Standard	Various	Hornby	2024
BR Conflat wagon	Various	Hornby	TBC
BR Mk 1 horsebox	Various	Hornby	TBC
21ton mineral open wagon	Various	Hornby	2024
CDA china clay hopper wagons	Western	Hornby	TBC
HAA Merry-Go-Round hopper wagons	Various	Hornby	2024
KFA container flat wagons	Various	Hornby	TBC
MHA 'Coalfish' ballast open wagon	Various	Hornby	TBC
'Seacow' bogie ballast hoppers	Various	Hornby	TBC
TTA tank wagons	Various	Hornby	2024
VEA box vans	Various	Hornby	TBC
VGA box vans	Various	Hornby	TBC

TOTAL: 29 CARRIAGES: 18 WAGONS: 11

Everything You Need For Your Digital Model Railway

DIGITRAINS

DIGITAL MODEL RAILWAY SPECIALISTS

www.digitrains.co.uk

JOIN US FOR OUR DIGITAL OPEN DAY

Saturday 20th January 2024

10am - 5pm

Trade Stands, Demo Layout and more!

Listen to our latest DCC Sound installations here.

- Try before you buy
- Expert Advice
- Great Service
- Experience
- Major Brands
- Worldwide Mailing

We stock 1,000s of products from more than 30 leading manufacturers. Don't worry if you're not digital.

We're also a traditional model shop, holding all the major ready-to-run lines.

 @digitrainsltd   digitrainsltd

 digitrainsltd

15 Clifton Street Lincoln LN5 8LQ
(01522) 527731
enquiries@digitrains.co.uk

Specialists in DCC Controllers and DCC Sound

DIGITRAINS

We have a dedicated workshop team offering a DCC Sound and DCC non sound fitting service. Offering a huge range of exclusive steam, diesel and electric sounds available for Zimo and ESU Decoders.

We have a dedicated demo layout in our shop showcasing the latest and best in DCC Controllers. Customers are encouraged to try before they buy, and our knowledgeable staff will be on hand to demonstrate systems and offer advice. Helping you choose the best system for your layout.

15 Clifton Street Lincoln LN5 8LQ
(01522) 527731
enquiries@digitrains.co.uk

Just laying it out there...

...or on the tabletop, in the lounge, in the bedroom, in the study, in the playroom...

The Hornby TT:120 possibiliTTies are endless!

HORNBY® TT:120

Perfectly formed to fit into your life.

SCAN ME

Now available at selected stockists

For further information, or to buy online, go to **Hornby.com/HornbyTT120**

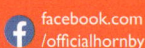 facebook.com /officialhornby
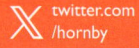 twitter.com /hornby
 instagram.com /officialhornby
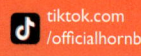 tiktok.com /officialhornby
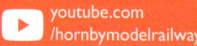 youtube.com /hornbymodelrailways
 Beyond the Buffers podcast
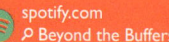 spotify.com Beyond the Buffers

BIG NAN'S LAST ADVENTURE

A book for kids about bereavement and saying goodbye to someone you love

Written & Illustrated by
Alex Waldron

This is the Fantastic World of Kernow County.
It is home to brothers Fred and Woody
and their family.

And this is the tale of how Fred and Woody said goodbye to their beloved Big Nan.

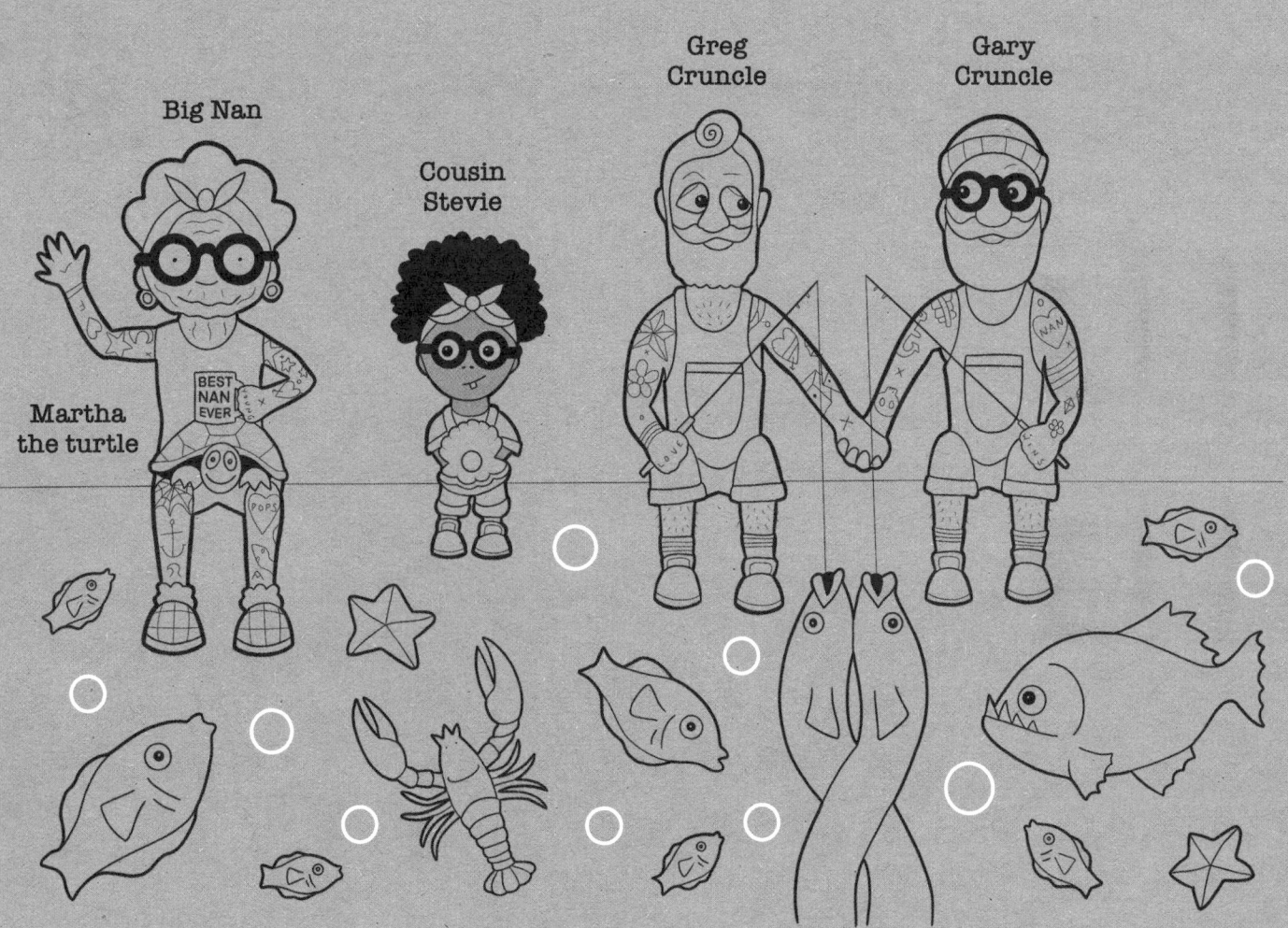

Big Nan is why we get up at dawn,
To check on the surf while we
Stretch and we yawn.

Every time we hope
To be first in the sea,
She's already there,
Surfing in the breeze.

From the moment she wakes
Till the Sun meets the sea,

Our Big Nan lives wild and free.

She's fearless and fierce and braver than you.

Big Nan's the reason we do what we do.

When we get to the top,
She's halfway back down
The mountain she knows
Like the back of her hand.

The crevasses and cracks,
The valleys, the peaks,
It's not the destination she loves,
But The Journey Nan seeks.

It's the fun on the way and the people she meets,
The adventures and challenges that fall at her feet.

She lives without fear
And with no regrets.

Every moment she gives
As much as she gets.

That's our Big Nan, so full of giving,
She teaches us all a lesson in living.

But today we got up early
And checked on the sea.
The surf was pumping
But the waves were empty.

We watched the great
Mountain and the valley below,
There was no sign of Big Nan
Or her tracks in the snow.

Big Nan has died.
She's not with us anymore.

You're no longer here.
Where did you leave us for?

PooPops says she's
Passed on from this place,
To a new adventure,
Beyond outer space.

Stevie says she's watching
From a cloud in the sky.
That sounds kinda cool,
Like being able to fly.

Our uncles the Cruncles say
She's returned to the sea,
Where she roams as a
Dolphin, wild and free.

Everyone believes different things and can't agree,
On what Nan's doing now and where she might be.

PooPops is crying but
Then straight after,
He remembers her smile
And cracks into laughter.

He raises his glass and
Shouts to the Moon,
Here's to my girl!
(And trumps a bit, too.)

But why are you laughing?
Don't you miss her so?

I do kids, says PooPops,
But there's something
You should know.

In this Fantastic World,
It's about the things you do.
And the way you treat others
Is how people remember you.

Big Nan we miss you
Wherever you are.

But know when we're sad
And stare at the stars,
Or walk on a wave or
Climb a great hill,

It's you who lives on
In both of us still.

A LETTER FROM BIG NAN
(Important stuff for little people and big people everywhere)

**To my dear Fred, Woody and Stevie,
And to all you other children and grown-ups,**

I've lived on this beautiful blue dot for many, many years. I've been lucky enough to love lots of people and lots of animals. But I've also had my share of very sad times when I've needed to say a forever goodbye to a much-loved relative, friend or pet.

Losing those I loved has taught me lots about death and grief. In this letter I want to tell YOU some of the things I have learnt, and hopefully my words will help you, too, once I'm no longer around to share this Fantastic World.

Getting Some Sad News

When someone dies, a family member or perhaps a friend passes on the sad news to other people. They may visit or telephone you. It can be a big shock when you find out that someone has died. You may feel scared and shaky. Some people start to cry right away, while others don't feel like crying. You might want to ask lots of questions, or you may want to be quiet and on your own. All of these feelings are OK.

Sometimes you might know that someone is very ill or getting very old and could die soon. Even if we know that a person is going to die, it is still a big shock when it happens.

(When someone dies, always explain to children what has happened as honestly as possible, using language that is appropriate for their age and experience.)

What Is Dying?

When a person or animal dies, their body doesn't work anymore. Their heart stops beating and they stop breathing. They can't see, hear, talk, move or feel anything. All living things eventually die. However, most people live for lots and lots of years until they are old – just like your Big Nan!

Sometimes a person has a serious illness. Doctors and nurses and their friends and family will try very hard to care for them and make them better. If it is not possible to make the person well again, they may die. If a person has a bad accident, their body may be seriously injured. Even though doctors and nurses work hard to help them, it may not be possible to fix the person's body and they die.

(Discuss with your child what is happening on pages 10–11. Big Nan is in hospital. She is laughing with the doctors and being brave, but PooPops looks sad because her illness is serious. On pages 12–13, Big Nan is back at home, but now she looks very unwell. It can be difficult and scary for young children to see someone change as an illness worsens. Try to discuss what is happening truthfully. If a child doesn't want to visit someone who is ill, at home or in hospital, that is OK.)

How Should I Feel When Someone Dies?

We can feel lots of different things when someone dies.

Upset	Sad	Tearful	Not tearful	Numb
Shocked	Wobbly	Shaky	Sick	Angry
Grumpy	Guilty	Anxious	Frightened	Sleepy
Empty	Nothing	Confused	Calm	Not sleepy

You might feel tearful one day, but grumpy or empty the next. Sometimes everyone around you is crying, but you don't want to. Different feelings may come and go. If someone has been suffering or was in pain, you may feel relieved. That is OK. It's very important for you to know that there's no right or wrong way to feel when someone dies.

The grown-ups around you may also be sad. They may act in ways that you're not used to seeing. They may cry a lot, shout or seem angry. All these ways of feeling are OK.

(Discuss the picture on pages 20–21 with your child. How are the different members of Big Nan's family feeling?)

Time to Talk

After a bereavement, it may be helpful for a child to speak to someone who has been specially trained to support children and young people who are dealing with loss. You will find a list of organisations on our Fred & Woody website: www.fredandwoody.co.uk

---

What Is a Funeral?

When someone dies, there may be a funeral or some other get-together where their family and friends remember them and celebrate their life. At a funeral, the body of the person who has died may be in a long box called a coffin.

People may cry and be very sad at the funeral. But sometimes people laugh, too. This doesn't mean they aren't sad or don't care about what's happened. Often people laugh because they are sharing happy or funny memories of the person who has died. At a funeral, people may sing hymns or play music the person liked. They may read poems, say prayers or make special speeches. Once the funeral is over, the body inside its coffin will usually be buried or cremated.

What Is Being Buried?

When a body is buried, it is put in a special hole in the ground called a grave. The grave is in a cemetery, which is a place where people are buried. Sometimes everyone stands around the grave. People may say goodbye, throw flowers into the grave or say prayers. Then the grave is filled with soil and it may be covered with grass.

Sometimes, after the funeral, a special stone is put on top of the grave. It will show the person's name and a message from their family. People may also put flowers or plants on the grave. You may have done this in your garden when a pet died, or if you found the dead body of a wild animal and buried it.

What Is Being Cremated?

When a body is cremated, it is taken into a building called a crematorium where there is a special fire. The body is burned until it becomes a fine powder called ashes. Some people keep the ashes in a little container called an urn. Other people scatter or spread the ashes on the ground in a place that was special to the person who has died, such as in a garden or at the seaside.

Remember! Being buried or cremated doesn't hurt the person who has died. They are no longer here and cannot feel anything.

Some children want to go to a person's funeral. But if you don't, that's OK. You could make a goodbye card, write a letter to the person you've lost or choose a special memento and ask a grown-up to put it into the coffin for you.

(Look at the picture on page 27 and discuss what is happening with your child. Young children don't always need to know all the details of what will happen to the deceased's body. But if they ask questions, it's helpful to be as clear and honest as possible to help them understand what's going to happen.)

Not everyone wants to have a funeral when they die. And that's OK, too. Then their family and friends might find another way to say goodbye, such as planting a tree in their memory.

Where Do We Go When We Die?

You and your family may have beliefs about what happens when we die as part of your religion or cultural traditions. Sometimes people have their own ideas. PooPops, Little Stevie and the other members of my family have lots and lots of lovely ideas. Thinking about the person you've lost being in a new place can be very comforting. But if you don't have any ideas, that's perfectly OK, too.

(*Big Nan's family have lots of thoughts about where she might have gone. See pages 18–19 and 20–21. Talking about where we go after we die can be very comforting for a young child.*)

When Will I Feel Better?

When someone dies, there is no set amount of time for feeling sad. It's OK to still do all the things you used to do, such as talking, laughing, eating and drinking, going to school, playing with your friends or taking part in your favourite sports or other hobbies.

It's OK to feel angry about what's happened, too. But don't hurt yourself or be mean to other people.

You may want to talk to a grown-up about how you're feeling or ask them questions about what's happened. But if you don't want to talk, that's OK. Sometimes it can help to talk about your feelings with a pet – cats, dogs and other animals are really good listeners!

You may always feel sad when you think about the person who died, but as time goes by, the pain will get better, little by little. Grief doesn't go away, but it changes and gets easier. There may still be times, however, when you feel sad again or the pain returns. You might feel extra sad on the person's birthday or when it's the anniversary of the day they died. But these occasions can also be good times to remember the person and enjoy happy memories.

Make, Share and Enjoy Memories

When someone dies, we can still love them, think about them and talk about them. Sharing memories, looking at photos or doing things you used to do together can feel comforting and nice. If you don't feel able to do that right away, that's OK.

(**Look at these pages in the book: 23, 24–25, 28–29. Big Nan's family remember lots about her. While reading the story and looking at the pictures, ask your child if they'd like to share some memories of the person they have lost.**)

Sometimes people visit the grave of the person who's died or another place that is special to their family. They may take flowers or other small gifts and place them on the grave. But if you don't want to do this, that's always OK.

At first it may be upsetting to remember the person. But in time, remembering them can be something you enjoy. Some people find being outside in nature in a garden, park, forest or at the beach helps them to think, enjoy their memories and feel calm.

You may miss the person you've lost for a long, long time. However, as time goes by, you may realise that you haven't thought of them for a few hours, days, weeks or even longer. Don't worry! That's perfectly OK. All your memories and the love you have for them will still be tucked away inside you. For always.

With all my love Big Nan

Time to Remember

There are lots of ways that we can remember a person we've lost. Often, making something connected to our memories can help us manage the feelings of sadness and grief. Visit the Fred & Woody website for tips and ideas:

www.fredandwoody.co.uk